How To Get People To Do Things YOUR WAY

J. Robert Parkinson

70725

NTC Business Books
a division of National Textbook Company • Lincolnwood Illinois U.S.A.

1989 Printing

Published by NTC Business Books, an imprint of
National Textbook Company, 4255 West Touhy Avenue,
Lincolnwood (Chicago) Illinois 60646-1975 U.S.A.
Manufactured in the United States of America.
Library of Congress Catalog Card Number: 86-60124

8 9 0 ML 9 8 7 6 5 4 3

About the Author

J. Robert Parkinson is an associate professor at Northwestern University. He has served as a consultant to numerous organizations and institutions. He was formerly Dean of the Institute of Research, National College of Education, and Director of Educational Research for Bell and Howell.

He is the author of numerous articles, and co-author with J. M. Boros, of *How To Get a Fast Start in Today's Job Market.* In addition he has been a consultant and trainer in effective corporate communications for professional associations, state government agencies, and private industry.

Preface

PLANNING TO WIN, OR—NEVER KICK A KANGAROO!

This book is about winning in the interpersonal encounters that make up our daily personal and business lives. All of us encounter situations of conflict on an almost constant basis. These conflicts are not physical or violent, but they are still conflicts. They represent situations in which two or more individuals have totally different points of view, different desires, different goals. And each one is going to try to get her or his own way.

When faced with such a situation, you must *compete* to achieve what you want. Your opponent won't just give in to you without some sort of fight—or he or she wouldn't be an opponent!

If you are going to have to fight, then you should know what weapons you have available and when to use them. You will want to use your strengths and pit them against the weaknesses of your opponent. You will want to pick the time and place for the encounter, and be sure you have a clear plan.

You must be sure you lead the way, however, so you can plan ahead of your opponent. You want time to choose the best time, place, and style for the encounter—the best, that is, for *you!*

As the title of this preface clearly states, "Never kick a kangaroo!" A kangaroo is far better at kicking than you are; so getting into a kicking contest with a kangaroo makes no sense at all—you will lose! That doesn't mean you must avoid the conflict, though. It just means that you must know better than to choose kicking as your weapon. Choose, plan, think ahead, so you choose the terms of the contest, and you won't get stuck playing kicking games with a kangaroo!

WHAT HAPPENS WHEN YOU SET UP A NO-WIN SITUATION

Let me illustrate with two personal anecdotes that show how a lack of knowledge of the opposition can be trouble. The first encounter took place when I was a new English teacher in charge of a freshman class of "average" high school students. I felt I possessed the fire of knowledge, and I had the feeling I was completely in charge. During one session, for reasons I can't recall now, I was being very glib with my charges who were getting a bit unruly.

I said to them, "This is a democracy, but don't forget that, in here, I'm King!" I thought that was pretty good, and the silence that followed convinced me that by all standards, I had made a point and was certainly in control. Then a youngster raised his hand slowly and said, in a very deferential voice, "May I get something straight?"

"Certainly." I responded crisply. "What is it?"

"You said you were King, right?"

"Right!" I replied

"And we're nothing, right?"

"Right!" I really had them I thought.

"O.K.," he concluded. "Then that makes you King of nothing!"

Silence—then laughter from the class. I was ready to respond—somehow. I was going to show them! Then I realized I had set up the situation; I had chosen the grounds for this confrontation. I was being clever in the use of words—and—the kids in this class were better at it than I was! I lost.

Never kick a kangaroo!

The second instance took place many years later when I was associated with the public school system in a suburban Connecticut town which served as a bedroom community for New York City. One of my first assignments was to prepare the budget presentation which was to go before a variety of committees and eventually before the Representative Town Meeting for adoption. The committees and the Representative Town Meeting consisted of citizens of the town, many of whom were doing their "civic duty" in addition to holding very responsible positions in New York City.

I developed what I thought was not only a very clear explanation of the budget, but also a very professional visual presentation. I had designed a series of transparencies for use on the overhead projector. They were colorful and clear; they employed overlays and progressive disclosures. They were so clear and so well done that there was no way that anyone could not understand the budget, the process, and the need for adoption.

We had more trouble getting that budget passed than anyone ever had at any time in the past! There were scores of questions and innumerable requests for more information, more justification. It was almost impossible to keep up with the volume of requests!

The budget was finally passed, and we took time to assess what had happened. The "pitch" was so good we didn't know why we had so much trouble. Then the answer came to us and it was very obvious: The "pitch" was too good!

It was slick! It had all of the elements of a well organized selling job. It was well scripted, well visualized, and well organized— just like a commercial!

Many of the committee members, remember, were working in N.Y. and many worked for various media organizations. Many members of our audiences were in the advertising business where the slick presentation is created every day. They looked at our presentation with the eye of the professional who deals with the "sell" every day. Our slick presentation put them on alert, so they kept asking for more information to find the hole in what we were selling to them.

There is an old saying, "Never con a con man." Our audience didn't consist of con men, of course, but a slick advertising-type presentation given to advertising professionals is in for a great deal of scrutiny. We were playing *in their arena,* and they were better at the game than we were.

Never kick a kangaroo!

The following year the basic presentation was the same, but we had learned our lesson well and made a few changes. There were no color transparencies, only black and white photos; no progressive disclosures, no overlays. It was just a plain explanation. We even built in a couple of errors that we knew would be "caught" by the audience. Each time the errors were pointed out they were corrected on the spot, by hand, using a grease pencil—not at all professional and certainly not visually appealing.

But the budget was passed in record time. We had elected not to play by the opponent's rules, but to create some of our own ahead of time. We set the arena for a simple, direct approach—where *our* strength lay, rather than theirs.

PLANNING TO USE WHAT YOU HAVE, TO WIN

These are but two isolated instances that illustrate the *need to plan* and *the need to use what you have* to get what you want. This may sound crude and antagonistic, but it really isn't. It is simply a way to say that you can control—to an extent—what happens to you, by looking ahead, and choosing from the alternatives on the basis of what will *work best* for you.

By thinking about the points in this book you should be able to be more successful in a variety of interpersonal encounters by *using your strengths where they will count.*

Conversely, you'll be more aware of the tactics and techniques others are employing—the very things that others often use to cause *you* to react the way *they* want.

The mechanisms by which people control others are easy to see once you begin to look for them. It is hoped this book will help improve the outcomes of your future encounters. But don't wait for the future. Start now—this very moment—and remember, if you want to play to win—*never kick a kangaroo!*

Contents

About the Author   *iii*

Preface   *v*

1   *The Elements of the Encounter*   *1*
Who wants everything their own way? The
subtle use of control mechanisms. The controller
and the controlled. Knowing exactly what you
want to accomplish. Articulate what you want.
Decide on the steps for successful completion.
Behavior patterns: adult or bit child?

2   *The Tactic and Strategy*   *7*
What tools do you have available? Planning the
encounter. Meeting the encounter. Control
mechanisms: your tool catalog. Emotional/mental
control mechanisms. Social control mechanisms.
Miscellaneous. In summary.

3 *Working with the Physical Factors*   *19*
Body language.   Costume.   Territory.   Eye contact.
Sex.   Props.

4 *Working with the Emotional Factors*   *45*
"Can—do attitude.   Affect the balance.

5 *Working with the Social Factors*   *71*
Vocabulary: "It ain't wha' cha say."   Jargon: anyone
can tell where I belong.   Name dropping: guess
who I saw today.   Citations: according to the
latest survey . . .

6 *Working with Other Miscellaneous Factors*   *91*
Writing that will be read.   The pen is mightier than
the sword.

7 *Coming to Closure*   *99*
Drafting rights: who says what and when.

8 *Synthesis and Conclusion*   *103*
What does all of this mean?   The concept of
competition.

9 *Epilogue*   *107*
Setting priorities.   Requirements and expectations.
A process checklist.   Review, and be good to your
self.   Planning ahead.

Appendix A: Suggested Readings   *123*
Appendix B: For Practice   *125*

DEDICATION

To all those who would like to make a practice of winning—in the ordinary conflicts and confrontations of everyday life and business!

1
The Encounter

WHO WANTS EVERYTHING THEIR OWN WAY?

There is a general acceptance of the belief that humans are social beings, and as such we strive to "get along" with others—to go along with them and their ideas. Upon careful exploration of that idea, however, it can be concluded that this is clearly not so.

It is not necessarily our nature to "get along," but rather to compete and to try and get our own way. Over thousands of years, many social mechanisms have been developed to enhance our ability to control other people in order to achieve our own desires.

THE SUBTLE USE OF CONTROL MECHANISMS

The concept of control described here does not include those actions which are crass, crude, or cruel—such as the use of personal violence or blunt weapons. Rather, this book is concerned with

1

the more subtle uses of control mechanisms that are applied within the context of society—with its blessing and encouragement. The techniques are not taught in any formal sense. Often those who are most adept in the use of control mechanisms are not even aware of their application, and those who are controlled don't understand why they feel and act as they do.

THE CONTROLLER AND THE CONTROLLED

It is of interest to note that during any given time, individuals may alternate between the role of controller and controlled. It is hoped that the ideas presented in this book will assist in adjusting behavior so that the reader can decide what role is desired, how to assume it, and how to evaluate how effective he or she is. For the purposes of this book we will assume that most readers are interested in improving their ability to control rather than to be controlled by others.

This brings us to the first principle of what can be called "control mechanisms." When you are planning to avoid kicking a kangaroo, *consider how you can set up controls and plans in advance.* There are many techniques, including two which are absolutely essential: *know what you want to accomplish* and *determine what steps are needed to accomplish it.*

KNOWING EXACTLY WHAT YOU WANT TO ACCOMPLISH

Please do not construe this statement to be the general idea of needing to know what one must do with one's entire life. That idea is too large and shifting a concept—too far removed from day–to–day activity. It is such a broad concept that it cannot be manipulated. Remember: every journey of a thousand miles must begin with a single step.

When you describe what you want to accomplish, look at the statement as if it were a single step, not the whole journey. You want to define what you want to accomplish *now* with this *single* contact at *this* meeting in *this* conversation.

ARTICULATE WHAT YOU WANT

You must decide, before any contact is made, *exactly what you want*. Then in very simple terms, state the desire clearly and in a manner that will allow you to observe your success—or your failure so you can learn from your experience.

Examine the examples below. In one–on–one situations you can be most successful when you decide for yourself in advance what you want the outcome to be:

"I want him to say 'Yes' to my request."

"I want her to say 'No' to another's request."

"I want my seat changed at the theater."

"I want to get on a different flight."

"I want my child's dental appointment changed to Saturday."

"I want him to redo this work, at no additional cost."

"I want her financial support for my project."

"I want him to hire me for this job."

Of course the specific questions and statements will be dictated by the situation, but the point is always the same. *If you don't articulate exactly what you want you'll never know how to go about getting it.* Further, if you fail in a given situation, without articulation you'll be unable to identify what you did wrong. Therefore, you won't know how to improve your performance the next time such a situation arises.

Many people have only vague ideas or notions of what they want to see happen and are often disappointed when things don't work out the way they intended. After the fact, they despair rather than understand that setbacks are not failures. Setbacks cause delays and changes in strategy, but *they can be dealt with if they are properly identified.*

DECIDE ON THE STEPS
AND SEQUENCE NECESSARY
FOR SUCCESSFUL COMPLETION

While it is clear that articulating the desired outcome in advance is essential, it is necessary also to realize that *sometimes a multiple-step strategy will be required for success.* Such objective planning goes hand in hand with the articulation of the goal since it forces logical, objective sequencing that will avoid the disappointment that can come from unrealistic expectations.

Developing multiple-step strategies follows the wisdom of the old saying that you must crawl before you can walk. To reach most goals, you must progress through prescribed sequences, or success will not come.

As you attempt to develop this new habit of using Control Mechanisms you must be prepared for some difficulties and a little trauma. The depth and duration will depend upon the strength of your commitment. Acquiring this new behavior is, in itself, a multiple-step strategy.

BEHAVIOR PATTERNS:
ADULT OR BIG-CHILD?

The process is much like the process everyone undergoes in working from childhood to adulthood. The only way to make that journey is to go through a difficult, upsetting, frustrating period called adolescence. The length of time spent in adolescence depends on many factors including culture, social status, sex, nationality, etc., but regardless of the length, without adolescence there can be no adult—only a big child.

As you examine your own behavior related to use of Control Mechanisms, and the behavior of others with whom you come in contact, you will discover many examples of big-child behavior all around. Such recognition, of course, is important in developing your strategy for control. If you are dealing with a child your tactic will be very different than if you are dealing with an adult. If you can identify big-child symptoms in an opponent, use them; take advantage of them. If, on the other hand, you are faced by a real adult don't waste time on child-like tactics.

One other significant consideration is the recognition that your opponent might be neither a child nor an adult but is somewhere along the way on that road through adolescence. If that turns out to be the case, be prepared for irrational reactions. This is the mark of the adolescent, so don't allow yourself to react in kind. Two adolescents in conflict waste a great deal of time and energy in the elements of the contact itself with little knowledge of how to reach a conclusion. When confronted by an adolescent be prepared for a circuitous route to closure. If you have defined what you want to accomplish, you can afford to take a circular route to get there simply because you know where you are going. The chances are excellent that your opponent has not gone through the articulation process, so he or she will have a much greater chance to get lost in a rambling situation. When your opponent gets lost—you win! Because you know the destination, you can determine the course and make the necessary and appropriate corrections. In short, you control!

2

The Tactic and Strategy

WHAT TOOLS DO YOU HAVE AVAILABLE?

At this point it is appropriate to explore some of the major categories and specific tactics related to Control Mechanisms.

They are broadly arranged into four categories: Physical, Emotional/Mental, Social, and a General Miscellaneous. It is important for the reader to keep in mind that these are generalizations, and each individual must make modifications as befit his needs. The guidelines offered here will work, but they are just that—guidelines. These are not foolproof scripts that will produce identical outcomes for every person in every situation. A little of your own imagination is not only essential, but also it will make this new behavior fun, productive, and uniquely yours.

The Physical

Let us begin with the Physical. It is easiest to observe, and it is something you can build upon right away. If you find physical aspects which seem negative for you you can immediately consider what compensatory behavior you will emphasize in order to overcome this perceived limitation.

Although of necessity, we will look at physical characteristics individually it is important to remember they are all interrelated in each of us. Each person must bear in mind the total image he or she wants to develop as all of these separate elements are combined.

Size

In our society, the tall person often has an edge over people of "average" size or "small" size, in many situations.

Studies conducted on the behavior of one group of personnel directors have shown a definite preference for hiring taller people over shorter people. Although this was found to be true both of men and women hired, it was less often true of women.

Obviously there is no way to increase your actual height, but there are ways to influence the perception of your height.

If you feel your height needs attention, what can you do?

Posture is the element that can be adjusted. Simply stated, *"Stand up straight!"* or *"Sit up straight!"* Not stiff, but rather poised posture is best, with the head high and the back straight—just the kind of good posture we were all taught as children, but which many of us have ignored with the passing of the years.

Good posture produces a visual impression of self-assurance and knowledge of the situation. If you are perceived to be "loose" or "sloppy" or "careless" about the way you present yourself, the extent of your impact or control on others will be reduced.

Standing up straight will also reduce your waistline in some cases!

Poor posture signals you as a target for your opponent by making you seem vulnerable. Likewise, look for it in your opponent; it could be a sign of weakness that you can turn to your own advantage.

By not displaying a firm image, you indicate lack of strength. If you really feel weak or inferior in a situation, and reflect such feelings, that can quickly lead you to failure. If, on the other hand, you "act out the part" of looking strong and self-assured, two things will likely happen. First, your opponent will react to what is seen as firmness or strength. That's a point for you! Second, if you practice the outward appearance, you might find yourself believing you really are strong! In this way you can "feel" yourself into a productive new behavior.

Remember, however, that such action is directly related to the basic principles stated earlier: you must know what you want in each situation. Once you articulate the desired outcome, you can marshal your resources to accomplish it. But how do you go about doing that? It's not as difficult as you might think.

PLANNING THE ENCOUNTER

Before the encounter takes place, go through it in your mind—rehearse it in advance. Play a little script-writing game with yourself, although preferably *not* word for word. If you rely on that, and the other party doesn't respond with the "right" words from your script you might get confused and lose the advantage. It is better first to think of the points the other party will make in response to and in opposition to what you want to accomplish, and then to decide the sequence of points you will make. Be sure to state clearly—and in this case the precise words—what you want to accomplish. Next, it is important to set the stage by visualizing where the encounter will take place.

Will you be standing at a counter? Sitting at a desk? Will you be in a private office? Whose? Will you be in an open service facility? Indoors? Outside? Simply stated—before it takes place, try to imagine and make yourself aware of as many of the components of the situation as possible.

The chances are excellent that your opponent will not go through such a mental process, the actual situation will be new for the other person, but not for you! You have already made your mistakes, and corrected your behavior. Your opponent is going to make mistakes during the meeting—when it counts—and you're going to win.

To repeat, "Plan your meeting, and then meet according to your plan." Having the advantage of knowing what your plan is allows you to get over the first few very important minutes—or seconds—of your encounter. You know how to start because you already know precisely what the outcome is to be and what the steps are that will get you there. It is easy if you set off in the correct direction.

MEETING THE ENCOUNTER

Now comes the encounter. Let us suppose that you just walked into the private office of a person you are to meet for the first time, J. L. Smith, the chief engineer of a production company. What do you expect to find? What kind of image do you have of J. L. Smith? How have you structured the encounter?

Plan for Contingencies

It's easy to answer those questions, although the answers probably reflect a stereotype. You may expect a man to be J. L. Smith. But, J. L. Smith may be a woman. So when you devise your plan be sure it includes contingency plans. As was indicated earlier when we discussed word-for-word scripting, you could put yourself into a trap by not considering possible alternative situations. Don't let a totally unexpected event throw you.

Of course, there is a way to avoid that possibility, and it is part of your planning process. Find out in advance as much as possible about your opponent. A phone call, a review of trade literature or a company newsletter, etc. can help, as can information from others who have been in situations similar to what you will experience.

Simply stated—*don't take anything for granted*, and *don't leave anything to chance.*

Now the confrontation—meeting—is taking place. This is the time! What will happen? What are the factors mentioned so far? Size and posture. You can see immediately how your sizes compare. Do you have a physical size advantage over J. L. Smith or must you look up to her or him?

Size up the Situation

The *degree* of difference between you and your opponent, something we haven't mentioned yet, can be significant. If you are within a couple of inches of each other, making height difference almost a standoff, you should concentrate on other strengths. If you are quite a bit shorter you *must* concentrate on posture and bearing. If, on the other hand, J. L. Smith is markedly shorter than you, don't over-emphasize your height. If the person is made more aware of stature, he or she may become defensive or, worse, antagonistic.

Now what are your initial moves? Walk into the room, shake hands, say hello, and sit down when invited to do so. How can these exhibit strength and lead to control?

The Simple Process of Walking into the Room

When you enter, do so with an <u>air of assurance</u> which can be exhibited and established by posture, pace (rate of movement) and grace. A straight but not stiff or rigid stance is always best. You don't want to look like a military guard, but neither do you want to appear as though you are casually strolling along a beach. Holding your chin high and slightly forward will set the stance for you. When you hold your head high, positive things happen: you appear taller, you establish eye contact and your voice improves.

Speed or Pace

Be aware of the speed with which you approach J. L. Smith. Don't rush! If you do, you'll appear tense, and lose control. Then too, by moving too quickly you run the risk of tripping on the rug, bumping into something, or displaying some other awkward movement, again losing control. On the other hand, don't amble like John Wayne in an old movie. Close the distance at a comfortable and reasonable speed.

Shake Hands

Now for the hand shake. It's done every day, but so often it is done poorly. A shame because a good handshake is easy, and says so much. It is the first and often the only physical contact we have with other people. It should work to our advantage and benefit.

Two words describe a good handshake: brief and firm. It is a clasping of hands and holding that position for a brief moment. It is certainly *not* a continuing "shaking" or "pumping" action. The contact is made, held for just a second or two, and released. That second or two, however, is extremely significant! The clasp should be just that, a clasping—not a mere touching. The feeling of strength in the clasp should communicate confidence. It should not overstate, so as to suggest a contest of strength. That could cause a negative reaction you don't intend.

The position of the clasp is also important. Be sure you clasp the full hand and not just the fingers or high up on the thumb. This proper placement of the clasp happens easily if you are somewhat deliberate. Don't be in a great hurry. Be sure to position your hand fully in J. L. Smith's. Once that is done, squeeze slightly, and release. Sounds easy, and it is; but it's very important. It is often done poorly!

If Smith behaves in exactly the same way you do, you are, so far, on an equal footing. But if J. L. Smith doesn't shake hands in this manner, and you do, already an advantage is yours.

Using Your Voice

A simple "Hello" or "How do you do?" is appropriate during the handshake, but while simple, it should be clear, and it should indicate a relaxed, confident attitude. Even if you don't feel confident, don't let on to J. L. Smith.

Just as your walk should be well paced, so should your speech. High speed is confusing, and it signals tension. Force yourself to speak at a comfortable rate and with a well-modulated voice. Listen to what you are saying, and how you are saying it. Be aware of how you sound. We will deal more particularly with the voice in a later chapter.

Won't You Sit Down?

Finally, when invited to be seated, notice the chair to which J. L. Smith directs you. Is it in a place that will put you in an equal position? A chair in an equal position is as high as the one in which the other person will sit, and it should seem to be as firm. Sitting in a big overstuffed chair, you could end up with your knees against your chin, an awkward position which could certainly put you at a disadvantage. Sometimes occupants of offices will arrange the furniture so as to put their chair in a higher place, and, therefore, a more powerful and commanding position. If you have a choice, pick a chair that will put you in a good position relative to J. L. Smith. If you have no choice, sit straight on the edge of the chair, and be sure to use the good sitting posture techniques,— deliberate and confident, like your handshake!

Suppose that J. L. Smith is a woman. What should you do differently than if you found J. L. Smith to be a man? Nothing! All of the techniques are just as appropriate for a female Smith as a male Smith. If you the reader are a man, of if you are a woman, you will find these techniques work equally well for you.

Practice Makes More Confident

It is often difficult to practice handling these encounters by yourself, so how can you get ready for them with a minimum of time spent? Certainly a tape recorder can be of great assistance for working on your voice. Use one often and be critical of what you hear of yourself—but then be complimentary to yourself, too, when it is warranted. Get used to how your voice sounds, and practice speaking clearly, and in a well-modulated tone.

If you are in a position to do so, use a video tape recorder and camera to evaluate your appearance and movement. Although this technique will be commonplace in the near future, equipment is not yet available on the scale that audio tape recorders are. If you don't own the necessary components and you really want to use this evaluation technique you can rent what you need from a local supplier, or perhaps borrow it from your local library.

Observing Others in Encounters

Opportunities to observe role models in these initial encounter situations are also readily available. Motion pictures and television portray many such meetings. The next time you see one on the screen watch it carefully. Ask yourself a few questions about what is going on. Pay attention to voice, to position, to posture, pace, and grace.

If you work in a setting that provides the opportunity to do so, watch other people in encounter situations. Another place to watch initial encounters is in restaurants. Watch business people greet each other, and watch as new members join already formed groups. What happens? What movements are observable? Do yourself a favor by watching what goes on around you. See it, don't just look at it! Think yourself through situations, and then practice whenever you can using whatever feedback techniques and devices you have available.

By taking the time to analyze the elements of a situation before you enter it, and by stating clearly what you want to result from an encounter, you'll have an excellent chance of being successful. You may not win every point every time, but your "batting average" will be very high.

Remember, most people don't go through such steps and preparation. If you do, you have an advantage at the very outset.

Now, use it!

CONTROL MECHANISMS: YOUR TOOL CATALOG

Knowing how to control situations and encounters, you'll be able to recognize techniques being employed by others attempting to manipulate and control you. Knowledge of these techniques can enhance the communication process and improve interaction. It can also heighten the competition to determine who is in control.

What then are the various factors which affect control of a situation? Which can you use? Of which should you be aware because they might cause you to act in a way contrary to your best interests?

Simply phrased: *What are the Control Mechanisms?*

For purposes of this book they fall into four categories: Physical, Emotional/Mental, Social, and Miscellaneous.

The Physical

We already discussed certain aspects of the physical, namely size, voice, pace, grace and posture. Others to be included are:

COSTUME—Business suits, military uniforms, ethnic clothing, casual vs. formal.

TERRITORY—The feeling that "This place is mine."

EYE CONTACT—Look, but don't stare. Where to look. How to avoid looking blank.

Affect the Balance

As long as your opponent thinks to have the advantage, he or she will use it. An opponent who thinks you can be pressured or intimidated will grow overly confident. If you can encourage this confidence so that it goes too far, the advantage will be yours, however. Just lead a person to where you want to go, and when this point is reached, conclude the discussion by stating what you want—even making your point by using your opponent's own words.

One of the best examples of this tactic is used by a friend who always dresses moderately, speaks softly, and describes himself as "just a poor country boy." He is so non–threatening that people relate very easily, and thinking they are controlling a contact become willing to go along with him in his stated direction. He is so good at using this technique, his particular brand of Control Mechanism, that this "poor country boy" is worth millions! He knows how to use what he has to get what he wants.

SOCIAL CONTROL MECHANISMS

Within social settings there are many things we can use to our advantage if we are aware of their impact. It is also possible that we will unknowingly react to these same devices ourselves if we are not aware. Social Control Mechanisms include:

Vocabulary

What we say. The words we use quickly categorize us in the minds of others. This doesn't mean we should use "big words" all the time, but we should use the appropriate words for every situation. In "My Fair Lady," Professor Higgins said that Liza Dolittle was " . . . condemned to the streets . . ." because of her speech. When the speech was changed, Liza became a different person.

Utilize good speech—to communicate your confidence and command of language as well as the ideas in the words themselves.

SEX—When and how sex differences or similarities can make a difference. What kind of "game" may be played.

MOVEMENT—What your body tells others about you.

PROPS—Using a briefcase, clipboard, folders, and other objects.

EMOTIONAL/MENTAL CONTROL MECHANISMS

Under the major category of Emotional/Mental Control Mech anisms we will discuss the following:

"Can Do" Attitude

If you convince yourself, and believe the accomplishment of th task is possible—you'll do it.

Territorial Relationships

This is the behavior which is influenced by the feeling that "This mine. I own this turf." Feeling comfortable in certain places pro vides an opportunity to boost your sense of self-confidence whi you are there and then, when you are ready, to transfer that con dence to other areas.

Picking the Contact

Often you can select the method of contact—or confrontation. might be, for example, by phone or face to face. Pick the one mc comfortable for you and the one you feel will be most productive

The phone might be a better way to start with because y can prepare notes or a checklist to keep in front of you during t contact.

Jargon

This separate part of speech is a specialization of vocabulary. Every business, profession, ethnic group, neighborhood, etc. has certain words or phrases which are used by those who "belong." If you wish to compete in a given arena, learn the jargon of that group or individual—and have it ready to use in encounters. If it is a specialized jargon, or highly technical, your knowledge of it can be a surprise which will work to your advantage.

A caution—use jargon words carefully, and don't overdo them. Be as natural as possible. Overuse of jargon will signal only superficial knowledge—leading to the feeling that you are a "phony." You want your opponent to think you know a specific business intimately, and you can do so by using that jargon, but be careful! Don't try to give the impression that you are an expert, if you are not.

Name Dropping

As with jargon, you can use names of people who are of importance to your opponent in your conversation. You can command attention—and possibly respect—by letting your opponent know what and who you know. But, again, don't overdo it, and don't overstate your knowledge or your acquaintance.

Citations

Most people state positions or conclusions by saying "I think that . . ." and usually "that" is sufficient. However, use some knowledge of the field you are discussing by quoting, paraphrasing, or citing from a specific source. Say "According to so-and-so . . . ," or "According to State Law such-and-such." Now you have introduced additional weight into the conversation. It is no longer just you and your opponent; you now have an ally—in your specific knowledge. If your opponent can't call on similar support for her or his side—you win!

Obviously using such a tactic requires that you do some homework. If you intend to cite an expert or quote from a book you must be sure of what you say. Prepare carefully by reading and listening. Gather and analyze your information before you try to use it!

MISCELLANEOUS

Other mechanisms can be combined in a miscellaneous category which deals with a wide variety of techniques including the following:

Note Taking

Refer, during an encounter, to simple notes you have prepared. (This is often a way to enhance the "according to . . ." tactic.) Refer to notes while you cite a source, and you will have a tremendous advantage in any encounter. Write down—in plain sight—what your opponent says when making a specific point. This is a tactic which will put your opponent off guard, and it will also enable you to read back what has been said—if it becomes advantageous for you to do so.

Concluding Remarks

At the end of an encounter, state the conclusions—the agreement—in your own words, and get your opponent to agree with the statement. This technique often allows you to get what you want just by saying it! Often your opponent will agree with your total summation even though he or she may not have gone as far with a particular point in summing it up. Using your own words, therefore, often both insures and assures your position.

SUMMARY

In every case these same tactics can be used by your opponent—so learn them well. Use them well, and beware when they are being used by the other person. Don't be manipulated or controlled by these mechanisms. Let that happen to others.

Finally be sure to pick the right time and right tactic so you will . . .

Never Kick a Kangaroo!

3

Working with the Physical Factors

BODY LANGUAGE

There is an old song lyric that says, "It ain't what you do, it's the way that you do it."

The way you move during a confrontation can help you win, it can also contribute to your defeat. People are judged by their position, their reputation, by the clothes they wear. Well, people also judge others by the way they move their bodies, or what is often called *body language.* During an encounter, movements are important.

In any kind of face-to-face exchange it is necessary to be aware not only of what you say, but also of how you look while you are saying it. The way you move contributes importantly to your overall appearance.

Picture for a moment a comic cliché—Mr. Peepers, Pantaloon or Casper Milquetoast, a theatrical character who speaks rapidly in a high-pitched voice with hands trembling and eyes nervously looking from side to side. He hardly presents an image of one who is in charge of the situation. He looks nervous and scared, and will have a difficult time winning in any confronta-

19

tion. He looks nervous, he feels nervous, he seems an easy target for his opponent. This is a picture of what you don't want to do. You don't want to present that kind of target, so what can you do?

All You Have To Do

First of all, remember that in most interpersonal situations you probably don't present that kind of picture. Since you can talk with your family, your friends, and your co-workers without appearing nervous, you know that you are capable of smooth, controlled movements. All you have to do is transfer those movements from the comfortable situations to the more tense situation of a confrontation.

How To Do It

Saying, "all you have to do . . . " doesn't help much, does it? It is an understatement, and most people would say that's plenty! Once you try it you may find it's not as difficult as you imagined.

Consider how you can control the movements, and therefore, control the situation. First, be sure you are prepared for the confrontation. Do your homework.

When the time for the confrontation arrives you are likely to feel pressure, stress, tension, and a dozen other similar emotions. This is very natural. As each of us reacts to confrontation, certain physical changes take place in our bodies. The moment we engage in a confrontation there are changes in our chemical balance. Even the anticipation of a confrontation can trigger the change.

"Flight or Fight"

Quite simply, adrenalin is pumped into the system, and we go into "high gear." We can't control the flow of adrenalin, but we can control the effects it will have.

When that dose of adrenalin is pumped into the system, the feet are the first part of the body to react. This "Fight or Flight Syndrome" has protected people from the time the first carnivore loomed into human view. Adrenalin impels us to want to move away from a source of pressure. But if we move away from a confrontation, we will lose. What to do?

Channel That Adrenalin!

Resist the urge to flee, and concentrate on controlling your feet. Keep them still. If you are standing, place both feet flat on the floor, slightly separated. Stand straight with your weight evenly distributed. Don't walk around; don't shift your weight from one foot to the other; and don't sway back and forth. *Stand still.*

If you are sitting, forget that the chair has a back. Sit forward! If you place both of your feet flat on the floor, they won't move around. The simple tactic of keeping your feet still helps you harness that energy triggered by the adrenalin; you have moved one step closer to winning.

Direct That Energy!

Now you must concentrate on directing all that energy to the rest of your body. But be sure to let your body move just as freely as you do at home, talking around the kitchen table. Although some people feel that to control means to be still, that just isn't true. To control means to be sure your body moves in productive ways which will contribute to your winning the confrontation. If you allow your body to move freely it will invariably do the right thing. It won't let you say one thing and do another. The organism just doesn't work that way.

Try a little test to demonstrate this. Say aloud, "I want to show you three things," and hold up two fingers as you say it. Notice how hard you have to concentrate to put up only two fingers rather than three! Your body will not trick you into doing the wrong thing if you just allow it to move freely.

And Take It Easy

An additional way to control "Flight or Fight" movements is to *take your time.* If you deliberately concentrate and focus your attention on each specific thought, you will be unlikely to succumb to rapid movements. Remember to speak only when you're looking at the other person's eyes; *give yourself license to be quiet.* You will discover that your movements slow down considerably and you will be able to "punctuate" your words with pauses. The resulting quiet will also give you time to organize your thoughts.

When you refer to your notes, for example, take all the time you need. Be deliberate in your moves. Your adversary will wait. Should he or she become impatient and try to hurry you along, establish eye contact and simply say that you'll find the item in a moment. Then return to looking at the notes in silence.

Similarly, if you wish to write a note, do so without rushing. Rushing will only start an acceleration which could lose you control of the situation.

Pay attention to self-assessment. Evaluate how well you are doing throughout the encounter. In an instant you can check on how well your system is performing.

In Summary—The Four A's

Your movements should be controlled in such a way that you can communicate that you are:

ATTENTIVE

ACTIVE

ALERT

AGGRESSIVE

Concentrate! When you are in the throes of a confrontation, that activity should have your highest priority and be given your greatest effort.

If you apply the above "Four A's" you will stay on track for winning that confrontation.

COSTUME

*From the time we are little children, we hear this
admonition in one way or another. "You can't
judge a book by its cover."*

Maybe not, but people do it to each other all the time! Consciously or unconsciously we all make judgments about people based on the way they look. Shopping in a store, riding on a bus, or walking down a street, we form impressions of the people we see. Some we would like to meet; others make us anxious or afraid just by the way they look, and by the clothes they wear.

A character in a play or a movie has a certain personality, and part of the fulfillment of that personality is accomplished by the way the character is made to look. The makeup and costumes are significant elements in the communication of the character. As we "people watch" on television, in films, plays, photographs and in daily life, we develop and reinforce concepts of the ways in which certain types of people dress.

Sure, this is a stereotype, but the world is full of stereotypes. Bankers are conservative; musicians are flashy; artists are sloppy. We've all heard these, and to a degree there is some truth underlying such generalizations. Certainly there are many exceptions to each generalization; but, the generalization does provide a basis for the way we look at the world and the people in it.

As we mature, our world-view broadens. We come to certain conclusions which seem to us to be reasonable. Since we think we know how certain types of people dress, we become confident that by observing how a person looks we can determine what that person is like.

Despite what we have been told, we conclude that, indeed, we *can* "Judge a book by its cover," at least until we have a chance to look into the matter more deeply.

Judging Books by Their Covers

We are all victims of this observational shorthand; most of us use it without even thinking.

Quickly, what kinds of people look like this:

1. A thin woman wearing horn-rimmed glasses, a plain black dress with a high white lace collar, and hair pulled back tightly into a bun.

2. A long-haired young man wearing an earring and carrying a guitar.

3. An overweight middle-aged man in a wrinkled suit, carrying an attache case.

4. A tall, straight-backed young man with very short hair, shaved around the ears, wearing pressed, starched fatigues and highly polished boots.

5. A muscular, clean shaven young man with blown-dry hair, wearing trendy designer jogging clothes.

6. A middle aged woman with gray hair, in a navy blue pin-striped suit, briefcase in hand.

We could go on and on with similar stereotype descriptions, and we would expect pretty uniform agreement in identifying these types of people.

Your first ideas were probably something like this:

1. a librarian or teacher

2. a rock musician or folk singer

3. a salesman

4. a soldier

5. a wealthy playboy

6. a lawyer

These are stereotypes, to be sure, but nevertheless, they do occur to people when they make first judgments or identifications of people at first glance. These stereotypes may be way off target—Number 1 may be a millionaire art patron; Number 2 may be a college professor, and Number 3 may be a well known diplomat, and so on. But the point is, that their costume and general appearance give an impression that has certain connotations, and that is what you want to work with.

You want to plan the first impression you want to make.

Since we expect certain people to dress a certain way, when we see a particular type of appearance we automatically identify that person as a particular "type." We then expect certain behaviors and actions from that person. It's a quick, easy system; and most of us use it. We don't like to admit it, but we do.

When we do this, though, it means that we instantly reach a conclusion about someone we have not seen before. When we make such a judgment the person must refute or reinforce that initial impression through additional behavior. If the initial impression was positive, fine; but if it was negative, the person must overcome an obstacle, although he or she might not even be aware that such an obstacle exists!

Making Stereotypes Your Friends

How does this use of stereotyping relate to confrontations, and how does it improve our chances of winning them?

What do we look for regarding appearance when we are planning a face-to-face meeting?

The first rule is to determine what is important to your adversary. This is much more significant than being concerned with what makes you feel good. You already know about yourself, but the confrontation isn't with yourself; it's with someone else. And you have to win over that someone. That's where you must concentrate your efforts—on your adversary. What will impress that person? Overpower that person? Intimidate that person?

To Join or To Fight?

Once you know what is significant to your opponent you can determine more thoughtfully the way you want to present yourself. Although you may have many choices of how to look, let's examine two of them here.

First, you can decide to "fit in," to look just like everybody else in the environment. You can decide to look like your adversary. If that person always wears a dress or a suit, you wear a dress or a suit. If that person wears a hard hat, jeans, and a denim work shirt, you present yourself in a hard hat, jeans, and a denim work shirt. You will then blend in with everyone else, creating an impression that you "belong," which could help you in the confrontation.

Your other option is to decide to be in direct conflict with the other person. If your adversary wears a suit, you appear in the hard hat, jeans, and denim work shirt. If your adversary favors work clothes, you wear the suit. Such a contrast can be effective in establishing your independence or strength of personality. Depending upon the personality of your adversary such a show of strength can help your position, or it can hinder it. You must decide. Do this with great care! Rather than being overpowered, your adversary might be angered.

If overpowered, the adversary will give in to your demands. If your opponent is angered, however, you'll find yourself confronted by an even tougher foe.

Make your costume selection carefully. Select what will help you win. It is uselessly hostile to say to yourself, "This is the way I always look. I'm not changing now. If people don't like it, that's their problem." Don't do that; it won't help you win. It is an attitude that might make you feel good for a while, but it provokes you into setting up conditions that could cause you to lose. If that happens, will you feel as good?

This may sound like too much work "up-front." It really isn't. There are some general rules of thumb you can follow about clothing, and you already know them. You know how your adversary will look; and, therefore, how you should look to fit in or to be in conflict or contrast.

Remember, *determine what is most important to you*. What do you want? To make a statement and to feel good temporarily? Or to win? If you want to win, do the advance planning, and take the steps necessary to be successful.

You can always change your clothes after you have gotten your opponent to do what you want!

For Example

Here is an example of what I think is a misplaced emphasis. I was observing a counseling session recently in which a woman was sharing her feelings about being angry. She was angry about being told what to do and what to wear. She described herself as a "Liberated Woman." The situation about which she felt so strongly involved an upcoming job interview.

It was for a job she wanted very much. What would she wear to the interview? She preferred pants suits, while the employment agency representative suggested that she wear a "nice dress." She objected to being told what to wear, and she objected to "a company policy that required women to wear dresses." Indeed, there was no such policy, but she had jumped to that conclusion. Further, she was also angry at the agency representative who told her to wear the dress. "What I wear is none of the agency's business or concern."

But the people at the agency were telling her what she should do to be well received at the interview. They knew there to be an expected mode of dress at the place where she would be interviewed; their comment was intended to be positive and helpful. The woman, however, angry at both the suggestion and the conditions, was looking to the counseling group for advice on how to handle the situation.

A significant question was raised. "Do you really want this job?"

"Yes," she replied.

"Then it's best to wear the dress if you want any chance at it at all. If there is an expectation that women will follow this type of dress code, and if everyone else complies, you then had best comply too, or you have no chance at all of getting the job."

Making a statement about no one telling her what to do in words, or implicitly in her dress, could jeopardize her chance of getting the job.

The personnel officer or interviewer might never tell the applicant she didn't get the job because of how she looked. Such a comment would invite a law suit for discrimination, and personnel people are far too aware of the law to run that risk. The non-conforming applicant simply would not be called for the job.

Of course, there are individuals to whom dress style is of great importance, symbolically or practically. If the right to individualism is very important to you, then you will not want to apply where you know a dress code exists. That would be . . . like choosing to kick a kangaroo!

Planning Your Look

In most situations, you improve your chances of winning if you are more like than unlike your adversary, and it is easy to find out what your adversary is like.

Visit the environment a day or so before your meeting. Or talk with someone who is familiar with the organization and its expectations. Finding out is easy and, if you keep your priorities straight, so is deciding what to do. If you really want to win do what will enhance your chances.

When you can make those choices without seriously compromising your principles, your task is easy.

What real difference would it make to that woman in the counseling session if she wore a dress or a pants suit? As great a difference as would be made if she did or didn't get the job based solely on what she wore to the interview? Only she could decide, but she should decide based on what contest she wants most to win.

Another Example

An acquaintance of mine related an incident that further illustrates how attitude and behavior can change based solely on how a person looks. Early in his career he was employed as a public school administrator while he was working on a graduate degree at an upstate New York university.

Because graduates of that university often sought teaching positions in the school system in which he worked, arrangements were made for him to interview applicants right on the campus. He scheduled date, time, and location via a telephone call to the Director of Placement. The day before the interviews, after he finished with his own class for the day, he stopped at the Placement Office to confirm these arrangements. The Placement Director was very cool to him and his questions, and as he was leaving she said to him, "And please be on time tomorrow!" What an unlikely and unexpected comment to someone who was in a position to hire her students!

But then he realized the problem. He was wearing his "student" clothes, not his "administrator" clothes. She really didn't pay attention to the fact that this "student" had the power to do the interviewing.

She reacted to his appearance, and reacted negatively.

The following day, when he arrived, on time, in his "administrator" suit and tie, she was charming, almost solicitous.

Same person, same place, different costume, different relationship. And, of course, being on time helps, too!

In Summary

Plan the way you want to look and the way you want to be seen. It can save you a lot of time, trouble, and tension. It can also help you win. And that's what you want from any confrontation.

TERRITORY

Never enter into a confrontation without being
familiar with the territory. Always reconnoiter the area
before engaging in any conflict.

When you are preparing for a face-to-face meeting of any kind try to get a feel for the space in which the meeting will take place. Remember, the other party knows the area and is probably very comfortable with it. You will be there for a relatively short time, and therefore, will be subjected to a wide variety of new environmental stimuli. Your adversary has a distinct advantage. So you must try to even things up a bit! How do you go about that?

There are many different settings in which meetings can take place. We can't cover them all, but let's look first for illustrative purposes at what can be done in a public area such as a governmental agency office. Second, let's look at what can be done in the offices of a private corporation.

A Public Place

The public offices are really easy. As the name signifies, the place is public, therefore, it's open. Certainly there are private offices and restricted areas in all public facilities, but you can get inside the main office area easily. Just walk in. Once you are there, look around. Take your time. Take in as much as you can.

Try to sense the atmosphere. Is it relaxed or tense? Friendly or hostile? Such an assessment can make you much better prepared to function in that environment when you arrive for the meeting.

Eliminate or minimize surprises. The more you can see, hear, touch, and smell about a meeting location before the meeting, the better you will do during the meeting.

It is never necessary to give your adversary the advantage just because the meeting is held on her or his territory.

Examples of public meeting places might be the City Council chambers or exterior meeting rooms, environmental committee meeting rooms, anterooms near court rooms, civic center meeting rooms, and the like. You will want to know what the acoustics are like in the room: can you hear clearly what is said in normal conversational tones? Is there loud noise nearby that interrupts conversation—an airport, or subway train, or other noise that might make a difference in your presentation of your arguments or speech? What is the room temperature like? Is it too hot or too cold? Ask a custodian or attendant if the room is always like that. Plan to dress accordingly, so that you are completely comfortable. What is the furniture like? Are the chairs light weight and tippy? Are they solid, and plain hardwood? Are there only soft, low couches into which your opponent might become too comfortable, and maybe tune out on what you have to say?

Set the stage to your advantage. In a public meeting place, you have the advantage of being able to adapt the setting a bit to suit yourself. Once you have taken a look at it, you know what to expect. You can arrive a bit early for the meeting, and open or shut a window, rearrange chairs so that you don't sit with blinding sun in your eyes, etc. If loud noise outside is a problem, you can even arrange a different meeting place beforehand.

If you have arranged the meeting to begin with, you will want to plan to make your opponent comfortable—but not too comfortable. Good solid chairs, a place for papers and writing, good light, right temperature, access to restrooms and, if you expect your meeting to be long, refreshments such as coffee or soft drinks may all be important.

If your opponent has arranged the meeting, you will want to be sure that you will have what you need—even if your opponent doesn't provide for it. If you examine the meeting place, and find it won't meet your needs, make your demands known. You may have special needs as well, such as a place to plug in a slide projector, or to set up a model. Make sure you'll have what you need.

A Private Place

Preliminary scouting can be a little more difficult in the facilities of a private corporation, but not impossible.

You can mention that you would like to visit the meeting room ahead of time, and this is usually quite possible. If you are not making your presentation to a group, but are only meeting with one person it may not be necessary or useful.

If you set up a visit ahead of time, use your time well. While you are in the reception area look for printed material that might be useful: annual reports, newsletters, corporate bulletins, and employee magazines all provide "inside" data you might be able to use. Look for names and title of people you might be meeting; look for listings of upcoming employee events, for recently awarded contracts, for new acquisitions, or for production notices.

If, during your confrontation you can refer to such information when it is appropriate, you'll strengthen your position and increase your chances of winning.

Remember to take notes and to refer to them during the meeting. Display your information and extensive preparation in a way that your adversary will see it.

The meeting might be on your adversary's turf but information will enable you to establish a firm foothold. From that position you can move more efficiently in the confrontation.

Setting the Stage to Your Advantage

Let's consider a couple of hypothetical situations. First, you want to take your family vacation this year in Arizona. There are four people in the family, and each of the other three have some ideas of their own, maybe already vaguely formed, about where they think the family should go. How can you set the stage for the meeting in which you'll win all of them over to your point of view?

You can already picture in your head the mountains, the deserts, the horseback riding, the campgrounds, the comfortable clothes you'll wear, the sunsets you'll see. And you want everybody else over on your side of this particular difference of opinion. How are you going to get them to see what you see?

Right—show them. You'll want to set up a comfortable time and place, when the family will be wearing comfortable clothes, and will have the leisure to think about what you have to say, and visualize what they will be able to see and do, on the vacation you propose.

You can set up a family meeting at the public library; reserve a private room, and spread out the books and magazines, or show the video of Arizona that you can get there. Or, if your family wouldn't be comfortable with that, you can gather up your information and brochures, maybe a video or some slides, using whatever equipment you have at your disposal, and get your meeting together at home at the kitchen or dining room table. You'll want to make sure you can have uninterrupted time and space—(can you turn off your phone, or put it on the answering machine? Choose an hour when people don't usually drop by. If the dog begs for attention, have a rawhide bone handy as a diversion.) Do whatever you need to do, to make sure you have all the advantages possible, to make your point and win. If one person in the family doesn't like horseback riding, plan ahead for that, too. Make sure you have something to offer that is irresistible to that person, so that the argument against horseback riding won't cost you the victory you want. When you have your props ready, make sure your setting is comfortable. Temperature, light, sound, fresh air, and refreshments are just as useful in winning over family as they are in winning over vice-presidents. Now, you can start your show. Show them sage brush, cactus, horses, opera companies, Indian reservations, turquoise jewelry, mountain streams—all the visuals you can get your hands on. Keep the opponents comfortable, absorbed and listening. Probably no one else is organized to this extent. You should be able to win over the group—because you planned and acted ahead of time to win.

Now, let's take a look at a second situation. Suppose you want to sell a company sales manager on buying a display booth for conventions, and you know that the sales manager bought a display not three years ago, and doesn't want to do it again so soon. You're setting up the meeting, since you're the person who wants to do the selling. What kind of setting do you want for your confrontation on this issue? Your opponent is uncomfortable already, with a three-year-old display, and no more money to get another one. And a salesperson pushing for a sale. So, you will want to make this opponent comfortable, first by implying that you are not pressuring at all. You want an easy atmosphere. Second, money is bothering the sales manager, so you want to minimize money, or at least make it seem far less important than other benefits. Third, once the sales manager is comfortable with you and the situation, you want to be able to demonstrate the advantages of your product to the point that the sales manager will want one, no matter what it costs. What kind of setting do you need? An office? Yours? You won't get the sales manager there. Theirs? They're already uncomfortable about seeing you. A restaurant? A nice dinner? Maybe. But there might be a setting that would be even more advantageous. How about their next exhibit? What if you show up at their booth, and help them set up? Listen to their problems with their present display booth. Ask what they wish they had, that would be easier to set up, provide more space, give more flexible display area. Talk, and help, with your shirt sleeves rolled up. Maybe this is only round one of a three-round fight; maybe you'll have to call again in a couple of weeks, and say, "Listen, I was thinking about your problem with the flexible display area, and I have something I think you'll want to see." If you can get the appointment, you'll have to set up your stage again— maybe this time, a restaurant would do the job. Then, the third time, after you have laid the groundwork of establishing trust and relaxed communication, and have had a chance to develop your arguments in conversation—then round three can take place at your office, where you can show the sales manager what your display booths do—fold up, knock down, form up in an L shape or a semi-circle, or a tall tower; all in less than 15 minutes with only the aid of a Phillips screw driver and one person weighing no more than 115 pounds. You can set the stage in your office so that you have no interruptions, the light, sound, furniture, noise level, and room temperature are right; and the sales manager is comfortable, and—it is to be hoped—overwhelmed with the effects of concentrating on your arguments, your product, your show.

What do you think would have happened if the sales manager had said, to your first request, "Yeah, okay, I'll see you. We've still got the display unit we bought three years ago, though, and it's plenty good enough for another three." And you had gone on over to their offices, and made your presentation. How much chance would you have to win?

Or, suppose you said, "We'll meet for dinner at the Benchley House. Have a good steak, enjoy the evening, maybe talk a little business." If the sales manager says yes, there will be more discomfort added. Maybe the steak sounded good, but now there's a feeling of obligation to add to his not really wanting to buy a new display. And you won't have had a chance to show advantages of buying your product. So in the restaurant setting, you may have a chance at winning, and you may not—it's about a 50/50 chance.

By choosing a setting with your purpose in mind, however, you have set up a situation where you're bound to win at least part of the battle. And by actually being at the exhibit, you have a chance to present more about your products as well. You may make the sale that day, and not even have to go for round two.

EYE CONTACT

Where do you look during the confrontation?

Does this seem like a simple question with an obvious answer? Of course you should look at the person you're talking to. But despite both the simple question, and the obvious answer, many people *don't* look at the person they're talking to. Instead, they look at the floor, the ceiling, the window, the desk top, their notes, finger-nails, shoe laces, or whatever else is available. In fact, a great deal of time is spent looking at anything but the other person's eyes.

In another section of this book, we advise you to look around the room to pick up clues about your opponent. Look for pictures, awards, souvenirs, and other items that will let you know what it is that your opponent values. Be sure to collect that data, but don't try to do that at the same time you're talking.

If you try to take in visual information from such a variety of sources while you are trying to send out your ideas, you'll find that a two-way flow of data exists which can cause you problems. You'll become more and more nervous, and you'll likely forget much of what you wanted to communicate.

While you are conversing, look directly at your opponent; you'll be able to think better, and your position will be stated far more clearly and persuasively.

Looking People in the Eye

Looking directly at the eyes of the person to whom you are talking doesn't mean staring, but rather that, when you are *talking,* you should look at those eyes; and when you look elsewhere, at notes for example, *stop* talking for that short period of time. If you develop the habit of talking only when you are looking into another person's eyes you will find that your ideas will be more clearly communicated, your speech will flow more readily and you will be much more effective in expressing your thoughts.

"Eye-Brain Control"

Communispond, Inc., a communications consulting company, re-fers to this process as "Eye-Brain Control." If your eyes move rapidly while you are talking you take in a great deal of visual stimulation. When your eyes "scan," every item in the environment; lights, chairs, windows and the world all provide visual information which the brain must process. While that information is being fed to you, your brain must still organize and process those outgoing messages which you wish to communicate. You are asking your brain to do two things at the same time.

Certainly the brain is capable of processing enormous amounts of information, but such double-duty demands its price. The visual over-stimulation created by scanning while you are trying to talk will result in increasing nervousness which will decrease your ability to think clearly.

If you concentrate on talking directly to a person and if you look at that person's eyes while you are talking you will reduce the visual stimulation thus controlling the nervousness you might otherwise feel. Such control will result in a substantial increase in your ability to think clearly.

More information on this technique is available from the offices of Communispond, Inc., 485 Lexington Ave., New York, New York, 10008.

To Look and To Look Away

When your opponent is talking, look at your opponent. Whenever and wherever possible avoid scanning the room both when you are talking and when you are listening. You will be receiving multiple messages, which might cause you to miss a significant point in your opponent's argument. Visual messages are so powerful that they can outweigh aural information. You can be easily distracted by light, movement or color. Be alert; concentrate on your opponent.

During the actual confrontation, words are the principal carriers of significant information. Don't risk missing those ideas because of visual distractions.

Certainly, break eye contact when you wish to write a note, but get back to the eyes just as soon as you possibly can. If you feel that a longer time is needed to write an extended note, politely interrupt to say something like, "Excuse me, but I want to be sure I have that accurately."

This tactic does a few things for you. It assures the accuracy of your notes. It breaks the flow of your opponent's ideas. It may also flatter or unnerve your opponent to see you writing the exact words that have been said. All of these factors can work in your favor.

Remember, you want to win the confrontation. Everything you do should be orchestrated toward that end.

In Summary

In order to win, you must be well prepared; and you must communicate your thoughts and ideas clearly. You must also follow the thoughts and arguments of your opponent, and look for conflicts and inconsistencies which you can challenge in order to support your position. Looking right at the eyes of your adversary will work to your advantage every time. *Try it!*

SEX

Confrontations differ with the sex of the participants.

Much has been written about sex roles and body language, which we won't try to recreate here. What does seem to be important in this regard is the recognition of the stereotypes which abound in our society.

Remember, the stereotype provides a kind of intellectual shorthand which can eliminate thinking. We must be aware of stereotypes that could affect us in a confrontation.

Big men with strong voices often simply overpower smaller, softer spoken adversaries. Even if the substance of what they say leaves something to be desired, the way they say it, and the way they look when they say it, overshadows that shortcoming.

Young and pretty women receive more immediate attention from men than do women of different physical characteristics. This may sound like a sexist comment, but ample evidence demonstrates it's often true. Studies have indicated a strong relationship between expectations which are based on physical characteristics of individuals and their actual performance.

What Are the Expectations?

There is another way of stating this which is directly related to planning strategies for a confrontation. We expect people to behave in a certain way based upon their appearance. Their sex is a part of their appearance. Like it or not, agree with it or not, men are expected to act in a certain way, and women are expected to act another way. The ways may be changing, but a difference remains. Argue about this issue at another time; attempt to change it as you will. In terms of winning in a confrontation it makes sense to recognize those factors that are operating in each specific situation, then to use them to your advantage.

Adjusting Your Actions

Think about how people behave, and adjust your actions accordingly. After all, it is much more productive to act on the basis of what "is" rather than on the basis of "what we would like things to be." This does not mean we should not work to effect needed change, it means we should, at the same time, put our energy where it will be productive at this given point in time.

When you engage in a confrontation, use the weapons at your disposal to win. Although we often hear about "winning the battle and losing the war," all wars are made up of series of battles. If you win the *important* little battles, you win the war! Concentrate your efforts where they will produce the greatest good.

Recognize and apply the statements expressed so well in Reinhold Niebuhr's often-quoted prayer, "Grant me the serenity to accept what I cannot change, the courage to change what can be changed, and the wisdom to know the difference."

That's excellent advice! If you're five foot four, there is no way you can make yourself six foot two, so don't waste your time stewing about it. Look for your strong points, and build on them. Use them to your advantage.

By using your strong points, perhaps your good voice, your coloring, your energy, or your intelligence, you can present an attractive picture that will gain the attention you want.

In Summary

You want to win, so use the weapons you have at your disposal. Don't waste time complaining about what you don't have.

It's much easier to build upon many little accomplishments than to try to build anything on a big complaint.

PROPS

In another section we indicate that characters in a play
need costumes to support and enhance their positions.
The same can be said for the use of props.

Props are aids to a theatrical production, and we should learn to use them to advantage in a confrontation.

We use props all the time, even though we don't usually think of them in that way. We don't realize the variety of objects that we can use to our advantage without our adversary being aware that we are using a theatrical technique.

Notes Are a Basic Prop

What kinds of props can we employ? Earlier, we discussed one at some length—notes, which make excellent props. Let's see what we can do with them and how we can make them work for us.

As props, notes can be used to focus attention, to institute a break in the flow of information, to provide thinking time. They can serve as a diversion or a way to shift to another topic. They can make you appear to be well prepared, and well informed. But, if you aren't careful, if you mishandle them, you can look foolish.

On the positive side, notes can focus attention. If, during your discussion, you wish to emphasize one of your ideas your adversary will become aware of its significance as you point out a reference which indicates that your comments are true and accurate. Quotations and citations, of course, are most valuable here. If, on the other hand, you wish to assure your opponent that you have found something significant in his or her presentation, deliberately write yourself a note on that thought. Remember to ask your opponent to pause while you get the quote correct. The simple act of pointing out a citation or a quotation or of writing a note will add importance to the identified items. They are treated differently from the other ones surrounding them so they stand out clearly. Once you have emphasized an idea in this way you may return to it as often as necessary and profitable.

Later in the meeting, you may wish to refer to the note which you wrote to capture your opponent's words. Quotations are powerful, and quoting your opponent's own words in support of your position can be devastating. As you write down your opponent's words be alert for inconsistencies in his or her position. If, for some reason, your opponent shifts position during the confrontation and you can point out that shift, you strengthen your position.

Using Notes

This is not a time for subtlety. Whenever you use the notes as props make the move obvious. Make sure that your opponent is aware that you are being careful, thorough, and meticulous. As your deliberate and repeated references to notes are seen, your opponent's perception of your strength as an adversary will heighten. You will have advanced your position considerably, by demonstrating that you are both well informed and well prepared.

Such evidence of data collection is a powerful tool. It not only demonstrates knowledge, but it also effectively counters an opponent's use of phrases such as, "I think . . . ," or "I feel . . . ," or "It seems to me that . . . ." Statements of feeling and belief can't compete with facts. If you have prepared well, you'll have more of those facts at your fingertips than you opponent, and you'll win.

What Should Your Notes Look Like?

For maximum effectiveness your notes should consist of a combination of items; actual documents such as statutes or policies, reports or copies of reports, typed material and your own hand written research. You will add to these your notes made during the meeting.

In all instances be sure to highlight selected portions of your notes. Yellow highlighter and/or red underlining indicate that these notes are working documents. Not only will your opponent be able to see how fully you have reviewed and assimilated the material, but also you will be able to find appropriate items with a minimum of effort.

And don't hesitate to let your opponent see all the highlighting and underlining! Without letting anything be read, you can be sure the materials are held in such a way as to display what you have done prior to the meeting. Add handwritten marginal notes to the typed and printed material. They can help you find appropriate items quickly, and their presence will further demonstrate the extent of your preparation.

For the most part these notes should look like working documents. Some will look neat; others will be messy. That's a good combination because you don't want to look like you prepared them only to carry into the meeting. Even if that is true, don't let it look that way. Remember, your notes are props, and props in a theatrical production look "real." Your material must also look "real." A good prop is not obviously a prop.

Props That Hold Your Props

A final question about notes as props: Where do you keep them, how do you carry them? Different businesses have different techniques so a little advanced scouting may be necessary to give you the specifics, but three options can be discussed briefly. You can find other considerations.

In most business organizations papers are transported in a brief case or an attaché case of some sort. These are comfortable, provide a writing surface should you need one, and they will enable you to have "back-up" material at hand. A case is essential if you must carry such bulky items as samples or displays.

Simple folders are often sufficient to provide quick access to a variety of printed material. Folders with pockets in front and back will enable you to organize the material into categories such as "evidence," "major points" and "back-up."

A third option is the clipboard, used regularly by some businesses and industries. It is even said that if you carry a clipboard in a military installation, you look as if you belong there.

In a sophisticated corporate or other institutional environment, you may opt for an elegant leather portfolio.

When you know where your confrontation will take place, arrange your notes using a briefcase, attaché case, folder, clipboard, or another container which you have identified as more appropriate. This prop will serve you well during the meeting.

Notes Can Be an Interruption

Now back to ways of using the notes we have constructed. We have described how they can focus attention, but they can also be used to break the flow of thoughts and ideas, a break which can be either in your thoughts or in your opponent's.

Why in the world would you want to break your own thoughts? Think for a moment. If you realize you are getting off the track, or if you are starting to develop a position that might be helpful to your opponent, you want to stop. But if you just stop you might look confused, weak and vulnerable as indeed you might be. *But* if you stop to refer to your notes, you have bought some time in which to rethink. Do this in silence. When you look up again at your opponent, refer to an item in your notes and put yourself back on track.

All of us, from time to time, have realized we were digging ourselves into a hole. The harder we tried to get out, the deeper we got. A friend recently gave me a simple but profound piece of advice for such a situation.

When you realize you're digging yourself into a hole—
stop digging.

You can't argue with that logic. Referring to your notes is a way to "stop digging" with complete control. While you are referring to your notes your opponent will be less likely to jump in, than if you just stopped talking and remained still. If your opponent does try to interrupt, fend off the interruption with a comment about looking for an item. Again, you are buying time and maintaining control.

Buying time provides you with the third advantage of using notes as props. You gain *thinking* time. A confrontation is a stressful situation, and it is often difficult to think under pressure. Your notes, your props, provide a tool to help your concentration. Use that tool to present your position as strongly as you possibly can.

Always use the tools deliberately and carefully. When you search for information in your notes, don't talk. Give yourself license to be quiet. When you are quiet, you can think. In just a few seconds of silence your internal computer will process information at an incredible rate. Give your brain those few seconds, and you'll be surprised at the results. Try it next time you are in a stressful meeting.

Notes Can Be a Diversion

Finally, use your props as a diversion a way to shift to another topic. Notes can help us to "stop digging" when we are getting ourselves into trouble; they can also help us apply a similar tactic when our adversary is building a strong case for his or her position in the confrontation.

Use notes as a tool to divert your opponent. When the opposing ideas are flowing well, and the evidence is leading to a clear conclusion, you can feel that your position is weakening. You certainly don't want to listen patiently until you have lost. On the contrary, you want to get back into the fray. But just interrupting usually won't work. Instead, it can lead to a totally unproductive shouting match. But if you have the notes ready, your interruption can be supported by a particular piece of evidence. And remember, if that evidence happens to be your opponent's own words, so much the better!

The point is this. By breaking into the flow of your opponent's ideas, referring to notes as evidence and justification, you have stopped things for a moment.

Once your opponent has stopped, you can refer to another point in your notes, working to move on to another topic. Winning is the name of the game in a confrontation, and controlling the flow of the information will increase your chances of success.

Never allow yourself to be maneuvered into a weakened position by an opponent who tries to talk you into the ground. If your opponent is pushing too hard, use the note props to break in and redirect the flow of information.

Preparation

It is here that preparation is very important. We've said it before: "Know exactly what you want to come out of this confrontation."

Write it out if necessary, and have it prominently visible to you as a part of your notes.

Your opponent doesn't have to see that statement, of course, but you do!

A caution. Having notes means having something in your hands. If you don't concentrate on using your body well you can run the risk of looking foolish and losing the battle.

Remember to move with confidence; use your energy to advantage and slow down. If you feel you are tightening up and becoming tense; stop talking, look at your opponent, and buy yourself some time.

Practice Makes Confidence

If you start flailing around and gesturing wildly, you won't be able to find your notes; you might even drop them on the floor. You might have a hard time recovering from that. You can reduce the chances of such an accident by employing another theatrical technique. Rehearse!

You won't have to go through every part of the presentation, of course, but ask yourself the kinds of questions that might come up during the confrontation. Or have someone else ask them. If you project and anticipate what might happen, and prepare a response you'll be less likely to be thrown by developments during the actual meeting.

Surprise can be one of your best weapons, but you don't want to be surprised by your opponent.

So *rehearse!* You might even enjoy it.

4

Working with the Emotional Factors

"CAN-DO" ATTITUDE

"I think I can, I think I can."

What you do and what you accomplish depend largely on what you believe is possible. Your state of mind can assist or detract in your quest to win in a confrontational situation.

Like the little engine that said, "I think I can, I think I can," we must have confidence in our abilities—or at least act as if we have confidence. We need to focus on our accomplishments.

By careful analysis and evaluation we can determine how to approach situations.

If we believe, "You can't fight City Hall," we won't fight City Hall. And if we don't fight, we'll certainly never win. But there are many times when we want to win, so what do we do?

Should You Fight City Hall?

Let's look at fighting City Hall. We'll use City Hall to represent any big formal structure. It might really be a City Hall, but it could be a state agency, a service organization, or a large company. Common to all of these, public or private, are a great many employees, each with a responsibility to carry out a specific part of the operation. In most cases, these employees know how to do their jobs one way and one way only; "By the book!" They expedite things. They move papers. They repeat activities again and again because "that's the way it's done."

When you raise questions you are told, "That's the policy." or "That's the law." If you're not careful, such statements can overpower you.

It's easy for any of us to crumble under the pressure of such weight. Law! Policy! Wow! And since employees recognize that such weight can be frightening to someone from the outside, they play on that fear.

In recognizing this situation, we can be ready for such comments, and in fact use them to our own advantage. There are two distinct courses of action we can take: one before the meeting or confrontation, and the other during the interaction.

Training for the Fight

Let's start with governmental agencies, although we'll relate the actions to the private sector shortly.

Before you meet with the "agency official" take the time to learn about the topic to be discussed. Read the law, statute, ordinance, or whatever rules might pertain. This might take a little time, but the advance preparation can have a strong impact on the outcome of the meeting. That's why you're doing it.

Shortly after I took my first assignment in a state government agency I was given an excellent piece of advice which has since served me well for many years.

> Learn the statutes that cover your area of responsibility. When you're preparing to meet with someone from another area learn the statutes that cover that area of responsibility better than the other person knows them. In the event of a disagreement—you'll win every time.

On the surface that might seem to be an overpowering task which would require a great deal of time and effort. Learning something better than the expert sounds like a lot of work. That might be true in some situations, but often a few minutes invested in preparation and research can be very rewarding.

A Successful "City Hall" Confrontation

A number of years ago an acquaintance of mine, whom we'll call Frank, had a confrontation with the Director of the Building Department of a sizable city. During a disagreement about a financial matter, the Director told Frank what "the Law" said in the case, certain that was all he needed to support his action. Needless to say, Frank didn't agree with the decision. That's why they had the confrontation in the first place.

By investing only thirty minutes at the local library, Frank learned about the law which covered the Director's responsibility. Frank simply read the statute—fully and carefully.

At the next meeting, held the following day at Frank's request, the Director again quoted the law—complete with Article numbers. But when Frank quoted the rest of the same law—complete with Article numbers—he won! What the Building Director quoted was true, but it was incomplete. Let us cite the specifics.

The matter concerned a building permit to put an addition on Frank's house. The permit cost $200. After the permit was acquired, a decision was made to cancel plans to build the addition. Since no work was ever done, a refund was requested. The Building Director said "No" to the request because the city ordinance stated that " . . . prior to construction a permit must be acquired." That was done, and according to him, the fact that construction was not started was immaterial. There would be no refund.

Frank's review of the ordinance at the library substantiated the Article quoted by the Building Director, but the very next Article said " . . . if construction is not completed a refund can be made. The amount of the refund will be the percentage of the permit cost equal to the percent of construction not completed."

Since none of the construction project was completed, one hundred percent of the cost of the permit was due. When the Building Director was shown the article, he immediately authorized the full refund.

He should have known that law—all the way through. Perhaps he did, but he quoted only part of it; and that part was beneficial to him. By learning about the law, Frank won the confrontation, and he got back all of his money. Without the visit to the library, and without the few minutes devoted to research, Frank would have lost. Because he took the time and expended the energy required to carry out just a little research, he won.

The phrase, "It's the law." can be overpowering, but be sure it's accurate before you give in.

What Makes It "Policy"?

Often, in business situations, we hear another phrase, "It's our policy to . . . " Clerks in stores will often quote "store policy" or "company policy." As soon as you hear those words, be on alert! The clerk is out to beat you down by quoting that ever-powerful "Policy," and who are *you* to disagree or argue with "the Company Policy"?

But the clerk who quotes "Policy" has handed you a very good opening. Tell the clerk you wish to see that policy—in print. If indeed it *is* policy, it should be available. After all, if it's not available—in print—how can anyone be expected to know what the policy is and be able to carry it out?

By this time the clerk will probably have called the supervisor/manager to "handle" you. Once again, simply ask to see the policy. Chances are excellent that no one will be able to produce it. You have every right, however, to see it, since its proported conditions are affecting your life.

If no one can produce the policy in writing, it just might be that what you're being told is policy is simply practice. "It's just the way things are done around here, and no one has ever questioned it before."

When the manager admits that, you have just about won the confrontation. You can now take many different tacks. You can claim that the store decision is unfair, prejudicial, illegal, unethical, or make many other similar—or stronger—accusations. In order to avoid a major problem, the manger will likely accede to your wishes—and you will have won the confrontation.

This approach usually works better in very large stores rather than small ones. "More people" means more organization, and that usually leads to more paper and more cracks through which a great deal of data can fall.

If you do business with certain establishments on a regular basis pay attention to how things get done. Ask questions. Employees will usually tell you what gets done "around here," or they will say, "Around here, everyone usually _____." Behavior is described in terms of what employees do, and have done for a long time, rather than on what a real policy manual tells them to do in a given situation.

Is It the Law?

In relation to the "Law," you should be aware that what is quoted is often not even the law. At least, with my friend, Frank, the law was quoted—although incompletely—but it was quoted. What you will often hear is not law, but either regulations or procedures. An explanation is in order.

Law—or statute or ordinance—is that precise language agreed upon by a specified majority of duly elected officials; local, state, or national. Law is the language that went through the legislative agency and was agreed upon to guide the behavior of the affected public.

The next step in the process is writing the *Regulations* related to implementing the law. The "Regs," as they are called, explain, expand, clarify and often limit the language of the law. They indicate what the law means.

Finally *Operational Procedures* are established and written to turn the words of the law into actions by those whom the law affects.

Sound like a straight forward and reasonable process? Wait! As one moves from *Law* to *Regs* to *Procedures,* the language often becomes more specific and restrictive. What started out as "You may . . . " in the language of the Law becomes "You should . . . " in the Regs. Finally, the procedure language says "You must"! And you must do it by the 15th of the month or you forfeit all claims, rights, and ownership, etc., etc.

It's a long journey from "may" to "must."

Duly elected and accountable officials create the law, but unidentified unaccountable employees write the procedures. Don't let anyone get away with simply saying "It's the law." Check it out, and do so with conviction. If someone quotes you the law, ask for a specific reference. Certainly, one who quotes the law should be expected to know the source.

If the quoter can't provide the specific reference you have weakened her or his position, and you are well on the road to winning the confrontation.

There is another very important factor to remember here. When your adversary quotes the source, always write it down for future reference. Very often a careful reading of a statute will allow for other possibilities. First, it might be possible to read another interpretation into the wording. You may find you can reach a different conclusion through the same words. Second, many statutes will state the *intent* and *expected action* in the very beginning of the section. However, subsequent sections or articles often cover *exceptions*, exceptions which can mean the difference to you between winning and losing. In other words, if at first you don't find what you're looking for, look again—and again!

A Confrontation with the Law

Let me illustrate. A neighbor was given a traffic citation because he turned into a street where there had been a "Do Not Enter" sign. The sign, however, was not on the corner; it was approximately 30 yards into the street into which he had turned.

As soon as he saw the sign, he stopped, backed out, and proceeded on his way. A police officer, who had been waiting nearby, maintained he didn't obey the sign and gave him a ticket.

All traffic citations have a box in which the officer must write in the statute which covers the offense. My neighbor went to the library and reviewed the statutes.

He found that Article 1 of the specified statute said, "Drivers must obey all posted traffic signs." Pretty clear! That certainly seemed to be justification for the ticket. Reading further on, however, my neighbor found this in Article 4: "If signs are not placed in such a manner so as to be seen by a reasonably careful driver, drivers cannot be expected to obey them." A possibly excellent defense that he could use!

A few questions of the city engineers revealed that the "Do Not Enter" sign had indeed been moved from its original location because of some construction work. It had never been returned to its proper place. Because the sign was improperly placed it could not be seen by my neighbor who was " . . . a reasonably careful driver . . . " The ticket was dismissed when he appeared in court.

He learned later that many tickets had been issued at that location for that "offense." He was the only one who had ever questioned the conditions. It had been a profitable location for the city and an easy place for police officers to guarantee they could issue a citation or two almost at will. They found it a good spot to make their ticket quota.

The day after the court appearance, however, the sign was returned to its proper location.

My neighbor used the information—the citation—to learn where to look in order to defend his position. He learned more about the specifics of the law than the officer knew—or wished to acknowledge.

In order to be successful with this you must think positively about your ability to pull it off. Think like a winner, and approach the research as if it were a game of hide-and-seek. Believe that you have as much chance of finding the truth as the next person does; then go looking for it!

In Summary

Don't take any quotation at face value. Listen carefully for the source of the quotation. If it doesn't come freely, ask for the source. Ask for specifics. Then be ready to respond with specifics. You'll find out that often you can " . . . learn about the statutes that cover your opponent's responsibilities better than your opponent knows them."

In the event of a disagreement, you'll win every time.

PICK THE CONTACT:
FACE-TO-FACE VS. LONG DISTANCE

Since confrontation must occur under certain physical conditions it is appropriate for us to look at some of these options. The word confrontation implies a strong interactivity. It will usually require an extended exchange of thoughts and ideas.

A confrontation can take place orally or through print. Letter writing is often the vehicle used to respond to a request or demand for information or action from a business organization. We receive letters asking us to provide information, send money, support causes, appear in court and the like. We must decide what response, if any, is appropriate. We'll discuss such written responses shortly.

Oral Confrontations

The sense of a confrontation seems to indicate a rapid interchange of words. It seems to fit best into talk, into debate, into argument. Within that context we'll look at the two choices: face-to-face conversation and telephone calls.

Telephone Confrontations

Let's begin with the telephone call because it provides some interesting opportunities. Some skills can be practiced on the phone first, before we "move up" to face-to-face activity.

First of all, consider the kinds of telephone calls you receive. If you receive a probing or hostile phone call from someone with whom you are certain there will be a confrontation there are two distinct choices which you can make immediately. The first is to engage the caller in the conversation. You can "go at it." Or you can choose the second option, and refuse to engage in the antagonistic discussion.

In order to "go at it" you should be certain you are prepared. If you expected the call, and you have done your homework in anticipation, go right ahead! If, on the other hand, the call is totally unexpected, and you are not prepared, don't get caught in this trap.

In the instance of the unexpected call, remember several things. The caller picked the time. The caller is prepared and is ready to engage in the confrontation. The caller may have even gotten "psyched up" for the call prior to placing it.

On the other hand, you might have been reading the paper, cooking dinner, writing a report, playing with the kids, or just relaxing. The unexpected phone call is a sudden invasion of your world, a sneak attack. You aren't ready for an instant reaction.

So don't try to provide one! If you are not prepared, don't participate. You have every right to tell the caller that it is impossible or inappropriate for you to talk at this time. Arrange for another mutually agreeable time when you can talk. If the caller objects to this, that's too bad!

You have as much right to determine the timing of the conversation as the caller does. If the caller tries to force the issue and proceed with the conversation you can always say politely, "I'm sorry, but I really can't talk now," and hang up! In this instance you certainly have the upper hand, so play it to your advantage.

If the conditions warrant, the caller will call back and seek agreement on another time, or perhaps you will receive a letter containing the details and the basic sense of what the caller wanted. There will probably be a request that you respond in some way. This brings us back to letter writing, and we will discuss that in detail a little later.

First, look at a situation in which you place the call. You may be calling at a pre-arranged, mutually agreeable time as described above; or in this instance, you might be the unexpected caller. How do you plan for placing such a call, and what advantages do you have?

"Get a Little List"

To start, make a list. Write out exactly what you want. Don't write a script. You don't have to write out every word you'll say, just write out the key words.

Indicate the reason you are calling; a Problem, a Request, a Complaint, a Correction. Whatever the reason is, state it clearly. You want to be very sure that the party on the other end of the line knows exactly what you want. A clear statement can set up the conditions for a productive outcome for you.

You might even be surprised to find that after such a clear statement the other party will agree right away. It happens sometimes, and when it does, it certainly saves a great deal of time and energy.

But in case you don't get that kind of instant agreement you must be prepared to move along with your demands. Have sufficient evidence ready to support your position. Write down the details which constitute the background. Dates, times, names, phone numbers and titles all can provide strength for your position. Get your facts straight. Be sure the sequence of events is correct, and that you place the right people in the right locations. You have time to prepare this evidence so take that time to line up your details with care and accuracy.

This might be the only opportunity you have to present your case, so do it well. Take sufficient time developing your position. Don't rush through the list. Don't allow your adversary to rush you through it with an "I understand" comment.

Even if your opponent does understand, the detail and the care which are evident as you present your position will be powerful arguments persuading your opponent of the validity of your position. A recitation of details can be unnerving to an opponent. That is exactly what you want. If your opponent becomes uncomfortable because you are so well prepared you have significantly increased your chances of winning.

Telephone Strategy

Remember, if your opponent is smart, he or she will interrupt you and say, "I'm sorry, but I can't talk now. Can we arrange another mutually agreeable time to continue this conversation?"

But although your opponent might do exactly what we would do if we receive an unexpected phone call, most people take the bait. They allow themselves to get drawn into a conversation just because the phone rang. For some strange reason people feel obligated to talk on the phone—even to a total stranger.

Most people won't talk to a stranger on the street, but they will on the phone. If an unexpected caller or vendor comes to the front door, they won't respond, but they will talk to that person on the telephone.

So be ready to bowl over your opponent as soon as the phone is answered. Take your adversary by surprise, and overpower him or her with your carefully prepared, researched, and presented listing of facts to support the action you desire.

Defensive Telephone Strategy

But, by the same token, if you receive that kind of call from a prepared adversary, don't participate. You are at an obvious disadvantage. Delay the confrontation by identifying that mutually agreeable, convenient time to talk. Then go prepare. Get your own information together.

If the confrontation is delayed, the worst thing that can happen is you will not be quite as well prepared as your opponent, but you will not be taken totally by surprise. On the other hand, you just might be far better prepared; and you will win.

In either case you will have had a strong hand in guiding the direction of the confrontation. And by knowing exactly what you want at the outcome, you will be able to use your evidence to support your movement toward that end.

If you don't know exactly what you want, you won't know if you ever get it!

Preparing To Meet Face to Face

Now it very well may be that the confrontation via the telephone is not possible. Perhaps that "mutually convenient time" must result in a face-to-face meeting. What then?

The physical conditions of the confrontation, of course, are different from the telephone conditions; but that doesn't mean that the preparation should be different. You will still need all the background information including dates, times, places, names, titles and phone numbers. All the information you would prepare for the telephone conversation is usable in a face-to-face meeting. In fact, writing out a list for the meeting can provide a valuable tool.

If you wrote a list in preparation for a phone confrontation, and your opponent suggests a meeting, use that same list.

Making Your Preparation Pay Off

When you are using a list during a face-to-face meeting, use it openly. Don't try to commit too much to memory. Don't make the notations small and difficult to read. Don't use little scraps of paper.

Use good size sheets and large type or writing.

Refer to your list and make further notes during the conversation. Create the impression that you know exactly what is necessary by careful and deliberate references to your notes. When someone sees an opponent refer to notes they begin to feel intimidated. This is especially true if the other party doesn't have equally complete and useful reference material.

As we have mentioned earlier, when you refer to those notes don't be in a big hurry. Take you time. If you try to rush you will have trouble finding the item you want. When that happens you start to fumble your papers, you start speaking more rapidly, you get more nervous, and you'll begin to lose your composure. With all that going on, you'll probably lose the conflict too. So slow down!

When you are looking at your notes do it silently. It's difficult to think and talk at the same time in this kind of situation, so do one thing at a time. Look at your notes; think about what they contain; and only then look your opponent straight in the eye and present your information.

Refer to those notes as often as you wish, or as often as you need to. This might be your only chance, so do it as well as you possibly can!

Remember the old adage, "Haste makes waste." It surely does in this kind of confrontation.

In Summary

A few general rules cover the various conditions associated with Picking the Contact:

- Don't be pressured into participating in a confrontation.

- Pick a time that is beneficial to you. An unexpected phone call doesn't require that you participate.

- Remember the telephone call is an interview. Being able to communicate via telephone is a wonderful technological advantage. It is difficult for most of us to imagine a world without telephones. However, that unexpected ring can shatter our solitude, our composure, and our schedules more quickly than any other device. Owning a telephone puts us at the mercy of everyone who might decide that a specific time is convenient to place a call to us. We have put ourselves at the beck and call of the whole world.

- Don't feel you are obliged to adjust your schedule to someone else's schedule.

- If you don't want to talk, or if you are unprepared to talk—Don't talk!

When the Roles Are Reversed

Now let's put the shoe on the other foot. Shakespeare wrote that during our lives " . . . we all play many parts." You can often be the receiver of those unexpected phone calls but you can place them to your advantage, also.

And do so, because if your opponent allows her– or himself to be pressured into the conversation you will be better prepared, and you will probably win the confrontation.

What do you do to prepare?

- Know exactly what you want!

- Make notes. Make a list of specifics. Know all of the who, what, where, when, why information.

- Get yourself "psyched up" to make the call. Organize your notes and pick a convenient time for yourself. Don't be concerned at this point about a convenient time for your adversary.

- During the phone conversation, go through the list carefully. Be sure you cover all of the points you fell are significant.

- Don't let yourself be rushed.

- Pick another mutually agreeable time to talk if your opponent can't or won't talk now. That might be another phone call, or it might be a face-to-face meeting.

To prepare for the next session, on the phone or face-to-face:

- Review your notes

- Gather more information if possible. Remember you have now lost the advantage of surprise. Your opponent now has time to prepare, so you have to be even better prepared.

If the follow-up meeting is face-to-face use those notes, and use them openly.

- Refer to the notes.

- Don't be rushed. If you try to read notes and talk at the same time you'll do neither very well. First read; then talk. The important factor is to win—not to finish on time.

- Write notes to yourself during the confrontation. Do this openly and deliberately. Let your opponent see this activity. The notes might be reminders to yourself about what you want to add to your presentation or they might be quotations from your opponent.

- A caution! Be sure you listen carefully. Don't spend so much time and energy writing notes on one part of the conversation that you miss important subsequent data.

- If you need time to write a note, say so. Ask your opponent to pause just a minute, and indicate that you want to be absolutely sure to write exactly what was just said. That tactic does three things. It gives you the time you need; it assures accuracy; and, finally it can unnerve your opponent. The interruption also breaks the opponent's train of thought, and can weaken her or his presentation by checking the flow of ideas.

- It is difficult for your opponent to object to such an interruption, because, on the surface, you are simply trying to assure accuracy.

- Finally, refer back to your notes as you reach the conclusion of the confrontation.

- Use your opponent's own words wherever possible along with your own to argue your position, to summarize and to conclude the elements of the initial disagreement. You increase your chances of winning and getting what you want.

Remember Why You're Doing All This

Never lose sight of exactly what you want. Before the confrontation, write out a simple statement of what you want the outcome to be. This will enable you to direct the conversation toward your goal. You will not be distracted by inappropriate material.

In order to win, you must know what you want and be able to tell when you have acquired it.

The chances are excellent that your opponent will not have taken such care in planning for the meeting, so you have another advantage. The magnitude of that advantage will vary during the confrontation. Be aware constantly for signs that the balance is shifting, and look for ways to keep it in your favor. Some of these techniques will be discussed in the following sections.

AFFECT THE BALANCE

As we just said, the balance of control will shift during the course of any confrontation. As each of the parties presents information in support of a particular position the degree of conviction will vary from person to person. First one side is strong, then the other side is stronger. And so it goes until conclusion.

Be Aware of Where You Are

The thing to remember in these situations is the need to assess such shifts and respond in such a way that your position remains stronger than your opponent's. If you constantly evaluate this balance you will be aware of when you are strong, and on the other hand, you'll know when you must do something to restore the power position which you have lost.

Let's look at how this balance factor operates, and at how we can affect it.

On Your Own Turf

The strongest position anyone can be in physically is usually being on one's own turf; home, office, whatever.

If you want to set up a meeting so it will be most advantageous to you right from the start, select your own office or home as the meeting place. Your opponent must come on to your "turf" for the confrontation. In sports jargon, you have the "home field advantage." It gives you an edge that your opponent doesn't have. You have all of the psychological props at your disposal. Your opponent has none.

If you need to acquire additional material or information during the meeting, it is available. You can go get it or have someone bring it to you right away. Your opponent must postpone or delay getting such additional material. Since your opponent can't match your new information with her or his own, you have an additional advantage, and you can keep moving toward your desired conclusion without hesitation or delay.

In many respects, because you control the environment, the setting, you also control the meeting.

On Someone Else's Turf

What about the times you must meet on an opponent's turf? How can you affect the balance and keep yourself in a position of strength? To be an equal contributor, and the eventual winner, you must employ some appropriate tactics to minimize your opponent's "home field advantage."

The best way to do this is to use what is there, on your opponent's turf, that can help strengthen your position. In other words, use something important to your opponent in a way that will help you get what you want.

You must try to learn a great deal more about your opponent than your opponent can learn about you. The more you know about an opponent the more vulnerable that person becomes, and the more likely you are to win.

Map the Territory

For purposes of illustration, let's assume you must meet your opponent in her or his office. As soon as you walk in, you can learn a great deal. The size and location of the office, and its decoration will tell you about the person's position in the organization. This can be important should you determine later that further follow up action is necessary. If, for example, the "office" is a desk located in an open area with many other desks you have found out that this person is just one of many who perform the same or similar functions. You have ample maneuvering room if it is necessary to "go to a superior" or person on a higher level.

If, however, you must find your way through a battery of secretaries before you get into the private office in the corner of the top floor you know there will probably be no higher level. Since this is the boss, you have limited follow–up potential.

Keeping Your Eyes Wide Open

Regardless of the office size, location, and decoration, there is always a great deal to be learned just by careful observation.

All of us place our individualism on display. Pictures, souvenirs, booklets and trinkets can speak volumes about a person's life, interests, hobbies and enthusiasms. Your opportunity to observe such items in the office will give you insights about the person on his own turf which that person can't get about you. You can be selective about what you communicate about yourself, but your opponent's environment speaks volumes. Be observant, and be ready to use what you observe.

An Example of Successful Detecting

Let me sight a personal experience which illustrates a way in which the environment contributed to the success of a meeting that had all the indications of a disaster about to happen.

Some time ago I was engaged to conduct research in a medium-sized city in central Illinois. Specific information had to be secured from a carefully selected group of people. The appointment schedule which was given to me had been developed by people familiar with the city and its power structure. Because the schedule was tight there was almost no flexibility. An important meeting was scheduled with the Chairman of the Board of the largest bank in the city. The appointment was scheduled for 4:30 pm on a Friday afternoon. An awful time for any meeting, but almost unheard of with this particular Chairman. Why he agreed to the meeting at that time is known only to him and to the person arranging the schedule.

The meeting was to take place in the Chairman's office at the bank. As soon as I walked into his territory, I found indications of problems. His desk was absolutely clear including an empty "out" basket. He had finished for the day! He looked as his watch as I came through the door, to see if I was on time, I guess. I was.

After saying "hello," he looked at his watch again and said, "Now, what is it that you want to know?" No preliminary conversation, no opening gambit, nothing but expediting the speedy dispatch of this meeting.

He waited—in silence—as I got out my notes and a questionnaire. He just stared at me. He was offering nothing to lengthen this encounter.

When I asked the opening general-information-type questions, he answered them curtly, briefly; and he looked at his watch again. The next few questions were answered just as briefly with "yes," "no" type responses. I was getting very little beyond simple basic data, and he was just going through the motions of completing the meeting. This interview was in deep trouble.

When the phone on his desk rang, he took the call. Usually I feel annoyed when a call is taken during "my time" in a meeting, but in this case I was thankful for an interruption which gave me some time to get my thoughts together. Perhaps I could figure out how to salvage this impending disaster.

For the first time I was able to look around the office for some clues which might be helpful in getting this man to open up. There had certainly been no time between walking through the door and asking the first question.

As I searched for information I saw the usual things: pictures of the family, framed letters from prominent satisfied customers, pieces of art work.

Then I spotted "The Clue."

A picture of a boat was prominently displayed on the wall. This was a significant clue not just because it was a boat but because of the kind of boat. I thought I recognized the manufacturer; if I were right, there would be a story behind its being here in the Midwest. It was worth a try.

When the phone call ended I pointed to the picture and asked, "Isn't that a Pacemaker?"

He sat up straight, and said, "Yes. How did you know that?"

I had touched a nerve!

I told him I had grown up on the east coast and had seen Pacemakers very often. They are made in the East, and for the most part they stayed there. The Pacemaker is a very distinctive boat with beautiful lines. I told him, truthfully, that I thought the Pacemaker was the most beautiful boat on the water.

Agreeing, he told me about his Pacemaker, how he got it to the Midwest, its position of splendor at his yacht club, his extended trips, and on and on and on. Not once did he look at his watch. Time was no longer important on this late Friday afternoon. We were talking boats. His boat. He was ecstatic!

In time he finally did look at his watch again, but now he said, "I'm keeping you here pretty late, and you haven't finished getting the information you need. How can I help?"

The interview went exceptionally well; I got all the data I needed as well as some additional insights which contributed greatly to the final interpretation of the study. It was one of the best interviews within the entire research project.

And that happened solely because I was able to affect the balance during that meeting. Finding that clue to what was important to that man provided the opening that got him talking. I was no longer an unwanted appointment looking for information; after I asked about his boat I was an informed, interested, interesting visitor who knew about something no one else in that area knew much about. And that something was very important to him.

I had brought something into his day, so he contributed to mine.

In this situation I was lucky in many ways; lucky the call came when it did; lucky he took it; lucky the picture was there; lucky I thought I recognized it; and most of all, lucky I was right. The part that was not luck, however, was my search for something, anything I could use.

How To Look for "The Clue"

Every office has clues if we look for them. They can provide a common ground for conversation. They can provide a diversion during the confrontation. If there is an element of commonality, of mutual interest, it is quite possible that argumentation can be turned into discussion. It's only when people are seen as different or in opposition that it becomes easy to do battle.

Personal items in an office provide such common ground, so look for them. They can be pictures of the family with kids the same age as yours, vacation photographs to familiar locations, sporting items, awards, or any of a host of other items.

Every office, every desk contains these clues, so look for them and, most important, use them.

The effective use of such information will contribute to the odds of your winning in the confrontation.

An Example of Choosing The Right Weapon

Let's look at another example of how the balance can be affected. This time we'll show how physical appearance can be used.

We all look different; some are big, some are small, but we need to assess how we appear to others and then use that appearance to advantage. This is a description of one person's ability to be successful in getting what he wants in a confrontational situation. We'll call him Larry.

Larry was very good at getting people to tell him exactly what he wanted to know, even when it was in their best interests to remain silent. As an investigator he was often called upon to provide information within some very high levels of corporate organizations. When clients needed to know just why things went wrong or in some cases why things went right, they turned to Larry.

Almost all of his investigations were carried out face-to-face. He was very successful in accomplishing his tasks although he frequently encountered people who were initially negative, uncooperative, even hostile.

What contributed to this success rate? His physical appearance, in addition, of course, to a sharp mind and quick wit. (Appearance may be important, but it certainly isn't everything.)

We have noticed that in most situations power is equated with size. Tall people may frequently have an easier time becoming successful than short people.

But Larry was short, thin, bald, and had a rather high-pitched, nasal voice. That's not very threatening or powerful at all you say? Right! But those were exactly the characteristics Larry used to affect the balance in his many confrontations with corporate executives who were big or tall or had strong voices. They were all used to dealing competitively with people who presented images much like their own.

Then along came Larry.

In his own words he explained his success. "No one is afraid of me. I'm small, skinny, and I sound funny.

"I'm not a threat to any of these people, so they tell me everything I want to know. They don't see me as an adversary because they feel they could beat me at anything.

"It might even be that they feel sorry for me because I'm just a little guy. So they help me out by talking about whatever I ask them. They never feel offended, and they certainly don't feel I'm taking advantage of them.

"How could such a little guy take advantage of the 'big guys?' "

By affecting the balance, that's how.

There are many ways to apply power. Direct confrontation doesn't always produce the results you desire. Larry disarmed his adversaries. When your opponent has no weapons, you win.

It seems paradoxical, but Larry's strength lay in his seeming weakness. He would never be "big and strong" physically so he made the most of the other strengths he had. And, he was very, very good at what he did.

Accentuate the Positive

Do a self-assessment. Be honest about your strengths and weaknesses. Don't try to copy the style of someone else because it might fail you. Observe others; learn from them; but don't try to simply copy them. Use your strengths, whatever they are, against your opponent's, whatever they are.

But be sure you select the weapons that give you the advantage, just as Larry did.

You Hear, but Do You Listen?

Even though you have picked the time and place, and used your best weapons to your advantage, there is yet another way to affect the balance in a positive way during a confrontation:

Listen! Listen carefully!

That seems so obvious. The reaction this comment receives most often is, "I always listen. How else would I know what the other person says, and when I'm supposed to talk?"

But the truth is that most people don't *really* listen during a conversation or a confrontation. They are more interested in putting across their thoughts and ideas than they are in hearing the thoughts and ideas of the other party. A University of Chicago researcher once described this situation as a "duologue." That's very different from a "dialogue."

A "dialogue" is when two people talk with each other. It is an interchange and exchange of ideas. A "duologue," on the other hand, is a situation in which the talking is quite independent of thought exchange. A "duologue" works like this. When one person is talking, the other is thinking about what he will say as soon as the first party is finished. Each person talks in turn, but neither listens to what the other is saying. Each is more interested in what he or she has to say than in what the other has to say.

When you want to affect the balance, listen to what the other party has to say. Those words might prove valuable to you. Listen carefully, and listen productively. You do that by concentrating on specific areas and items. For example:

LISTEN for Key Words

LISTEN for Key Ideas

LISTEN for Pressure Points

LISTEN for Maneuvering Room

LISTEN for Inconsistencies

Think over the items in this list, and then, let's develop these just a bit.

Key Words

Listen for Key Words. Every disagreement (and a confrontation involves a disagreement) has certain boundaries. Dollar costs, time frames, percentages, dates, and payment conditions are examples of such boundaries. Pay close attention to what is really required and expected. Don't get caught up in emotional issues or outbursts. Just listen for facts.

Key Ideas

Listen for *Key Ideas*. What does your opponent really mean or want? Again, don't let emotions cloud your judgment. Does your opponent *need* to win? Or simply not have to lose? There is a great deal of difference.

The urge not to lose can readily lead to an interest in reaching a compromise. When that interest exists, it's possible, and usually sensible, to search for a way to reach a mutually agreeable conclusion, one in which you both win.

Pressure Points

Listen for *Pressure Points.* Is your opponent under some kind of performance requirement? Must he or she complete this matter within a certain period of time? Is there a financial limitation or consideration? Must the resolution come quickly? Can the issue be resolved through compromise or must a supervisor approve any conclusion? Where is your opponent's place in the power structure? Who and where are your opponent's superiors? Can you get to them if necessary? Does your opponent think, or know, that you can get to these superiors?

Such information can be gotten only through careful listening to details and to the interaction of those details.

Maneuvering Room

Listen for *Maneuvering Room.* Pay attention for signals that will tell you there is a good possibility for a negotiated resolution to the problem. At the start of any confrontation there are two distinct positions, yours and your opponent's. As you present your evidence and listen to the reaction of your opponent's evidence, listen for indications that he or she could be interested in modifying that position. Even if your opponent won't admit it outright, a suggestion might be forthcoming that he or she would welcome discussion of a counter proposal. As soon as such a suggestion is observed, you must seize upon the opportunity!

Make a recommendation that will further your position. If your opponent wasn't interested in precipitating such a situation the possibility would not have opened up. When it is there, you have to recognize it, and move quickly.

Inconsistencies

Listen closely for *Inconsistencies.* Careful attention to details when your opponent is talking will often alert you to changes in the opposing position. Although maneuvering room conditions are usually suggested or initiated by the opponent for your use and action, inconsistencies are usually not deliberate. If, however, your opponent becomes confused and inaccurate concerning specific details of the problem, you can assume your opponent to be on unsteady ground. If the person had confidence in her or his facts, the position would be strong and solid.

But, if your opponent falters, and changes facts, he or she is vulnerable. Here is a point where your carefully taken notes can be used to your advantage. Writing down those "facts" each time they are presented can help you develop a strong argument right on the spot. When you read back your opponent's words, and you point out the inconsistencies and contradictions, you will place her or him on the defensive. When you've done that, you have almost won.

In Summary

Play smart and be alert. Listen carefully. Take notes. Use your opponent's own words to affect the balance of the confrontation.

If you do this consistently, you can't lose.

5

Working with the Social Factors

VOCABULARY: "IT AIN'T WHA'CHA SAY."

Professor Henry Higgins said that Liza Doolittle was " . . . condemned to the streets . . . " because of her speech.

As soon as we begin to talk people learn a great deal about us, or they think they learn a great deal about us.

We probably let them know where we came from, what part of the United States or from another country; our socio-economic status; our educational level; etc. Certainly we know it's possible to mask and modify these background elements, but in most people's cases, their speech is a dead give away.

Since people react so quickly and so strongly to the spoken word, that effect should be considered when we prepare for a confrontation. We should learn to pay close attention to how we talk. A tape recorder is an effective tool for preparing for any confrontation.

71

Hearing Yourself

So listen to yourself on a tape recorder. Get used to the sounds you make. Get comfortable with them.

Most people are surprised when they hear their own voices. "That's not me!" is a very common reaction. People don't hear their own voices, when they are talking, the way others hear them. It is physically impossible to hear our own voices in the same way others hear us.

When we are talking, our hearing mechanism receives the sound information in two ways simultaneously; through the ear and also through the bones of the skull. The hearing mechanism is connected directly by the various body parts to the vocal mechanism, and no one else has that combination except the speaker. Therefore, we won't sound the same to ourselves as we will to everyone else.

Our perception of ourselves is very different in many ways from the perception others have of us. We are a bit selective about how we see ourselves, whereas others are more realistic.

It has been said that, "We judge ourselves by our intentions, but we judge others by their actions."

We use different measuring devices with others almost all of the time.

Just as with audio recordings that don't sound like we think they should, so photographs do not look like we think we look. "I don't look like that! That's not me, is it?" are comments often repeated when people see their proofs.

There is a very simple explanation for why we think photographs don't look like we think we do.

Most of the time when we see images of ourselves, we are looking at something completely different from the way others see us. Most of the information about how we look comes from what the mirror tells us. That reflection, however, is not what everyone else sees.

The reflection reverses everything. The left and right sides of our faces and bodies are shifted around. The two sides are not exactly the same, so we see a totally different image in the mirror than others do when they look at us. The photograph, however, keeps the left and right where they belong; and through the photograph we see ourselves as others see us.

When preparing for your confrontation be aware of yourself as others will likely perceive you. After all, how they respond to you is more important than simply how you think you appear. Now let's look at some of the specifics of speech that deserve attention.

What English Do You Want to Speak?

For the purposes of illustration we'll limit our references to English, but remember something very important. Most of us, to one extent or another, are *multi-lingual in English.*

That concept is a critical one to remember as we prepare for and engage in any confrontation.

How can we be multi-lingual in a single language? Simple. As we consider what language is, we realize that in its simplest definition it is nothing more than a collection of agreed–upon sounds that convey a thought or an idea.

When groups of people agree that certain sounds stand for certain things, then that's what those sounds do. If, on the other hand, there isn't such agreement, then there is confusion; there is misunderstanding.

Using Today's Words

A humorous way to illustrate this, of course, is through the use of slang. Slang changes so rapidly that hard-core slang users must keep current, or they will be left out. Teenagers are the most frequent users of slang, so ask a local teen, or your own teen if you have access to one, what the current "in" slang words are. Ask what they were six months ago. You might find that many of the same words are used, but they now have entirely different meanings. Make a note of the current slang words and check again in six months. Sometimes parents will try to communicate with their kids by using familiar slang words but find that it doesn't work well, because what the parents thought the words meant is not accurate any longer.

If you plan to use slang, be sure it's today's.

Sounds Have Meanings
When We Agree They Do

Let's get back to language having meaning because people agree that sounds stand for and represent things and ideas. The sounds are intended to communicate, to move an idea from one person to another, to provide for mutual understanding.

Both parties in a two-way conversation, or confrontation, must perceive the sounds to mean the same thing to each of them. If a sound means one thing to one person and something else to the other party there is misunderstanding. Be alert for such a problem.

To illustrate: a teacher in Minneapolis was telling a story about some children having fun jumping around in a puddle of slush on New Year's Day. One child, new to the school, was listening to the story but frowning. He told the teacher that he was totally confused. The story make no sense to him at all, but the rest of the kids in the class understood. The teacher stopped and asked a few questions. The student had recently moved to Minneapolis from San Diego, which was the only place in which he had ever lived.

In San Diego, "slush" is the sweet crushed ice you buy in a paper cup and eat at the beach. It was beyond his understanding how anyone could gather up enough to jump around in a puddle of the stuff.

When he learned another meaning for the word he understood the story. The rest of the class, likewise, learned a new meaning for the familiar word, and they then understood the newcomer's complete confusion.

We all know that words can have multiple meanings; and that's part of the idea behind being multi-lingual in English.

Over the years we have been taught that certain ways of saying things are "right" or "wrong." English grammar books are filled with rules about the use of the language. "Always do this"; "Never do that"; "Use a capital letter here"; "Use a comma there, but never use a semicolon"; "Never end a sentence with a preposition."

Rules serve an excellent function because they provide a certain stability to a language. Yet the language keeps changing little by little. Even with the changes, people continue to communicate, but only if there is agreement about the meaning of the sounds. If there is such agreement there is communication. So, agreement between the parties can be more significant than the rules. Agreement is also the manner in which new words get into the language on a continuing basis.

Someone makes up a word, defines its meaning, others agree; the language is expanded. Lasar, Radar, Scuba, Pulsar. All of these words entered the language that way, and others follow every day.

So, rather than "right" or "wrong," what must be considered in communication, and certainly within a confrontation, is what is "appropriate" or "inappropriate."

Making Appropriate Sounds

That is where we become multi-lingual. Given a specific situation you use carefully selected words to convey an idea. If the conditions of a situation change, you use other words which are equally carefully selected. The language you use fits the situation. As situations change, language changes.

We all move from one situation to another, so we change language. We are multi-lingual. Or we should be.

The trick is to realize that varying situations dictate varying meanings. This doesn't mean that a speaker has to give up all prior acceptance of rules and become careless. On the contrary, it means that a speaker should be aware of the effects that her or his use of words will have on the audience being addressed at a specific time in a specific place.

Remember, the reason for the communication in the first place is to transfer a thought or idea from the speaker to the listener. What the listener gets and understands is the most significant factor.

The speaker must use what will be most effective, and in order to do that must be aware of her or his options. The speaker must then select the ones that will serve the immediate needs best, the ones that are most appropriate for the circumstances.

To illustrate: imagine the vocabulary that would be used in the locker room at half-time to describe how two football players felt about a player on the other team because he was doing a few things which they frowned upon. Even that description sounds a bit strange, doesn't it? They would probably have a few carefully chosen words to describe the player's actions, ethics, conditions of birth, racial or national heritage, mental prowess, and who knows what else. Whatever the words might be, they would fit that situation. They would be appropriate, in that they would communicate swiftly, accurately, and efficiently exactly what the players meant.

Now, imagine another scene later that same day: same players, but they are no longer in the locker room, and it certainly isn't half-time. They are sitting in a restaurant with their parents, girlfriends, and perhaps a team or college chaplain. When they tell the story of their planning session in the locker room, many of the words they use will be very different from the ones they used earlier in the day. The ones that were appropriate in the locker room just wouldn't fit now. These same words would now be inappropriate, and many of them might not communicate efficiently at all.

Similarly, the words used at the dinner table would have been inappropriate for the conditions that existed in the locker room.

These two players are multi-lingual, in that they use different languages for different situations. If they were not multi-lingual and if they knew only the locker room language it probably would have been a very short dinner party!

Keep this thinking in mind as you prepare for every confrontation experience. Ask yourself, "What is appropriate for this situation?" "What words will get my message across best?" "What do I have to say to get what I want?"

Modify to Fit

Modify your language to fit conditions, in order to accomplish your aims. Think about the people and the place associated with the confrontation. The environments change as you move from a store to a factory, to an office, to a board room, to a locker room, to the head table at a banquet, to a bar, to your own kitchen, and on and on. The language you choose to use will probably change a great deal.

Blending in and Contrasting

This is not intended to mean that you must become a verbal chameleon.

You don't have to change to blend completely into the environment, but you must be aware of your actions and your positions. Use your control of language to blend in when that will work best for you, but to stand out more in stark contrast when that will produce the desired results.

Whatever you do, do it with full knowledge, and with control. Whichever language you use, use it with purpose, and not just because of habit.

Pay close attention to your opponent. What language does this person speak? Which of your languages will be most effective in the confrontation? What words "fit"? What references will be most helpful? Should you, for example, talk in terms of millions of dollars, thousands of dollars, or dollars per hour? Will the conversation be concerned with "colleagues," "co-workers," or "buddies"?

Will use of a well-placed "ain't" provide emphasis, or will it indicate you don't know any better?

Once again, like the actor in a theatrical production, the selection and use of specific words will help develop the character, and they will communicate a great deal to your audience.

So, select carefully and consciously.

Non-Words and Spaces

There is yet another element of vocabulary to be explored. Just as you must use care in selecting your words so should you be aware of *non-words*.

Non-words can cause you a great deal of trouble. We all know what they are: "umm," "ah," "ya know," "like," and so on. They usually show up when you're not sure of what you want to say. We are so used to hearing ourselves making such sounds that we tend to fill in what could be spaces with non-productive noise.

In language there is provision for space. Space belongs between sentences, between words in a series, and between thoughts. It's not necessary to fill up those spaces. Further, if you constantly make sounds, you are depriving yourself of quiet time in which to think about what you are saying.

Silent Time

Silent time is thinking time.

Silence provides a way to pace and punctuate your presentations.

Give yourself license to be quiet.

You don't have to go on all the time. In fact, if you do it will be very difficult for your opponent to follow your train of thought. If you use a great many non-words they will become a distraction, or worse, an annoyance.

Your aim is to convince your opponents, not to distract them to death.

If at any time during your presentation you are not sure of what you want to say next, be quiet. Think. A split second is usually all you will need, and your opponent will wait. He won't even be aware that you are buying this thinking time. If, on the other hand, you fill up the space with non-words you will be broadcasting the fact that you don't know what to say next. You will be telling your opponent you are lost and confused, and that can be a fatal error in the confrontation. Never fall into that trap.

Non-words indicate a lack of preparation and a lack of confidence. Don't ever give your opponent such information. Non-words are just noise. They are non-productive. No one ever won a confrontation by using non-words. Noise is a distraction. Silence and selected pauses contribute to your presentation.

Control Your Choices

Be silent when that will be productive, and remember all the languages you have at your command. Use each of them selectively and wisely. Using an ill-chosen, inappropriate language will bring about your defeat. Don't beat yourself: beat your opponent.

If you don't think you are multi-lingual in English pay attention to how you talk in various situations. You'll probably see that you are changing quite often.

If you are doing this, okay; if you aren't, consider developing this skill. Listen to your speech. Use the tape recorder. Practice, and get ready.

It just might come in handy some day!

JARGON:
ANYONE CAN TELL WHERE I BELONG

*A specific form of multi-lingualism is apparent
in the use of jargon which is defined as "a
specialized vocabulary and idioms of those in
the same work, profession, etc."*

Jargon serves as a kind of verbal shorthand because selected phrases and words carry specific meanings to those who are informed and belong to that specialized work group. Once again it is necessary to know what words means within the field under discussion. "Overload," for example, means one thing to a truck driver, another thing to a computer programmer, and yet something else to an electrician.

Researching

When you find yourself preparing for a confrontation pay attention to the language of your adversary. Find out what is important to that person: learn something about her or his business before you make contact. How can you get such a working knowledge?

A little preparatory research will be of great help. Review the literature of the business. Every occupation distributes information about itself through a professional association or union. Monthly journals, newsletters, magazines, etc. are available at your adversary's place of business or at the public library.

Keep in mind the names of magazines in the particular field, and locate them in the library. Read to find out the language common to the people in the field; be sure you are familiar with key terms. Look for articles on current issues, and be familiar with the major parties or elements involved in any issues which affect your adversary, or the person's particular interests in the field. This can be of extreme importance, if it affects your opponent's ability to negotiate, or ability to buy or sell, or to grant you what you want in the confrontation in other ways.

Your research will also tip you off to the language-of-the-moment, in the sense that you will be able to pick up on the relaxed atmosphere that goes along with boom times in a particular business, or the reverse. If your opponent's business is in big trouble, or impending changes in the industry or business may constitute a major threat, you will be prepared for the heavier, more serious conversational style that will most likely be presented to you.

If you find such material at the opponent's place of business, you know he or she thinks it's important so you know where to concentrate your efforts.

While You're There . . .

In another section of this book we discussed visiting the place where the confrontation is to occur in order to assess the physical environment. While you are there look for printed information that is usually on display on a counter, coffee table, or information rack. Take whatever free samples are available. If some pieces must remain there, spend a few minutes going through them. You won't become an instant expert by any stretch of the imagination, but you will pick up some specific references you can use later.

Remember to make notes.

You know why you are going to meet with your adversary; you know the topic to be discussed; so look for items that relate to that topic. Don't devote time and energy at this point gathering general information. You can always do that later—after you have won the confrontation.

Look Selectively

Look for names, titles, dates of events that could be important, descriptions of these events, explanations of processes and procedures related to the topic to be discussed, reports on new developments or findings germane to your interests, etc.

With such specific topics in mind you can review a great deal of material in a short period of time, and you can strengthen your preparation.

You are, in effect, giving yourself a crash course in your adversary's business. Although he or she will continue to be more extensively informed than you, your knowledge of some of the specifics will probably come as a surprise; and, therefore, it will work to your advantage.

During the confrontation meeting your opponent probably will not have much opportunity to probe your background so he or she will respond most likely on the basis of the information you provide. When that information includes the jargon, the specialized vocabulary, the impression you create is that you somehow "belong." You are in the know!

A caution: just drop the jargon here and there in the confrontation. Use it carefully; don't over do it. Be as natural as possible. Overuse of jargon will signal superficial knowledge which could produce a feeling that you are a "phony." You want your opponents to think that you know their business, so don't give them a chance to probe, or they may find out that you really don't know all they thought you did.

The use of jargon is definitely one of those cases where "Less Is Better."

Focussing Your Research

If you're not sure of how to locate the magazines and publications that relate to specific businesses and occupations consult a publication directory in the reference section of the library. *The Encyclopedia of Associations* lists associations for almost every occupation you can imagine. There is information on size, location, structure, etc., but most important for you, it lists the titles of publications produced by each association. With that information you'll be able to locate specific issues quickly in the periodical section of your local library.

In addition, phone numbers are provided so you can call the association and ask for specific data related to the upcoming confrontation. You don't have to tell anyone at the association what you are doing, of course, but you'll be able to get all the information you need.

If you are pressed for a reason for wanting the information you can always use the vague response, "I'm doing research." There is no reason to divulge your purposes. It's a small world, and you have every right to privacy.

Acronyms and Abbreviations

Perhaps the most commonly used forms of jargon are the acronym and the abbreviation. Commit a few to memory so you can include them in the conversation. When you use them, however, be careful. Don't make a "big deal" of knowing them, but rather let them flow naturally within your remarks. Be absolutely sure you get the letters right, and that the reference is correct for the discussion.

Reasons for Knowing the Language

Remember at all times that the reason for collecting and using such information is to impress your opponents with what you know about their businesses. The more you know—or that they think you know—the stronger your position will be.

In all confrontations, you want to use your strength against their weakness. In this case that weakness is their lack of information about you.

In another section of this book, we discussed the value of knowing the laws and regulations which govern and direct a particular business and, therefore, govern your adversary. Your knowledge of the jargon related to such material will be of value because of the "verbal shorthand" we mentioned. Reference to a piece of legislation by its number, for example, can go a long way toward helping you win a point.

We'll discuss the use of such citations later in more detail, but for now let's simply reinforce the idea that *jargon, where used sparingly but precisely, will give you a perceived position of strength through your command of information.* Even small signs of being informed can create a significant impression, particularly when they include specific detail, such as jargon.

NAME DROPPING; GUESS WHO I SAW TODAY

As with jargon, names of people who are important to your opponent are important details to add to the image in your presentation. You can get your opponents' attention and respect by letting them know what and who you know. But, again, don't overdo it, and don't overstate the knowledge you actually have.

Where Do You Get the Names To Drop?

There are a couple of techniques that work well, in controlled and focussed name dropping. The first, of course, is to use the names of people you really do know and have known for a long time. Business associates, neighbors, classmates, etc. provide all good possibilities.

The key factor in the confrontation is to be sure the name is important to your adversary. If your opponent knows the person, that's good; but if he or she doesn't, then be sure to identify your contact by title or some other appropriate device. If just might be that you know people your opponent doesn't—but would like to.

Friends and Associates

Before your confrontation takes place make a list of people that you know who could somehow be of importance to your opponent. You won't use all the names, but there just might be one or two that could win some points for you. A few minutes of such planning can pay off in the midst of confrontation.

It's also a good idea to keep an active list of contacts just in case they can be of value sometime in the future. You never know when a confrontation will develop or what the topic will be, so a current list is always of potential use.

Have a card file or personal phone book as a working document.

Send a note to everyone once in a while, or make a phone call "just to keep in touch." When there is such an ongoing series of contacts over time, a specific request for assistance or reference is not seen as being out of the ordinary, and it will be responded to positively. It will be welcomed if it is actually just one more in a continuing series of friendly contacts. If you do this over time you will be pleasantly surprised about how many people you can call or refer to for assistance in a wide variety of areas, businesses, and professions.

So one way to drop names is to use the people you really know. But there are other ways to suggest that you have valuable or powerful contacts. This is not to suggest that you lie about your contacts; rather it is a way to use information.

Building Direct, or Indirect, Links

One technique is to quote authorities. The quote might come from a newspaper story, television interview, magazine article, or a radio commentator. Such references, brief as they are and as distant, nevertheless can be used to support your statements.

A second method is a little more creative. Perhaps the best illustration comes from a scene in the musical show, *How To Succeed In Business Without Really Trying*. The "hero" wants to work for a specific company. He stops the Chairman of the Board in the building lobby and asks for a job. The Chairman, quite annoyed by this bothersome request says, "Don't come to me about a job. If you want work here, go see Mr. _____ in personnel." Our hero goes to see Mr. _____ in personnel and says to him, "The Chairman of the Board told me to see you about getting a job here."

The personnel man, on hearing that the Chairman of the Board personally directed our hero to the personnel office assumes there is a direct link between the two of them. Our hero gets the job.

Now, everything that was said was true. In the telling, however, the facts took on a slightly different meaning. But, the result was exactly what our hero wanted. He had a goal, and he used techniques appropriate to achieving that goal. How can you do that?

One way is to set up the conditions by which you can honestly say that "President _____ told me to talk with you about this matter."

You can do this quite easily. First, find out who is your adversary's superior. An organization chart, a company directory, or a helpful receptionist, or a telephone operator can provide that information. Then call that person and ask the questions or request the information you desire. Or perhaps you will ask to be directed to the person you should talk to, to get those answers.

The superior will tell you to "Talk to Mr. or Mrs. _____" When you do meet, now you can honestly say, "Mr. or Mrs. _____ told me to talk to you." If your adversary happens to jump to the conclusions that are favorable to you as a result of your comment, so be it!

This technique requires some additional preparation, but the results are usually worth it. Some people feel this is deceptive, and in a way, it is. Some, therefore, won't use this technique. If you feel it is unethical, you surely should avoid it. We're not advocating it, but it is an option.

Who You Know

Often, we hear, "It's not what you know; it's who you know that counts."

Using name–dropping techniques will expand the perception of who you know, and that can help win the confrontation. After all, your opponent knows many, if not all, of the people you may name which could strengthen her or his position. You want to increase your strength in order to use it against your opponent's weak points. Name-dropping, therefore, can even up the contest, and perhaps even tip the balance a bit in your favor.

Just remember to be truthful, and do not overdo this technique. Be sure that you sound friendly, matter-of-fact, and direct. Name-dropping should be a subtle aid.

Where You've Been

In addition to people's names, don't hesitate to use place names too. If you can personalize information through evidence of visitation you are in a much stronger position than if your knowledge is only second or third hand.

Being able to say, "When I visited _____" makes you an instant expert. "During my trip to _____" means you have information your opponent doesn't have. "When I saw _____" clearly indicates you know first hand what you are talking about.

Use that power. Take advantage of what the visits and observations provide for you. If you have visited a country, a city, a factory, a farm, or whatever, and your opponent hasn't, your position is much the stronger. You can use that strength then, against the opponent's weaker position.

CITATIONS:
ACCORDING TO THE
LATEST SURVEY . . .

In confrontation situations most people state and defend their positions and conclusions by saying, "I think that . . . ," "I feel that . . . ," or "I believe that . . . " Such statements can weaken an argument. They usually don't carry enough weight to win any confrontation. They can easily be countered by the other party saying, "But I think that . . . " and offering an opposite point of view. When only personal perceptions are offered they can be dismissed quite easily.

You don't want your position simply dismissed out of hand, so what can you do? What options are available?

Again, a little preliminary research can provide valuable assistance for your confrontation. If there are any laws, policies, or corporate procedures involved, read them carefully.

Remember what we said earlier. "If you know more about the .rules that govern your opponent's actions, than your opponent does, you will win every time." Stating, "According to state law Number _____ . . ." will introduce weight. Unless your opponent can counter by citing another specific law or a different relevant section, you will win on that point.

Quoting an expert, likewise, introduces strength. You have an ally in presenting your argument. If your opponents don't have such allies to support their position, you will win there, too.

The essential element in this strategy, of course, is *your preparation.*

Focus Your Preparation

Keep in mind the goal you want to accomplish. Then look for specific citations and quotations that provide support for your position. You don't have to become a legal expert or corporate consultant to have such information available. Simply read and research with a purpose.

Never lose sight of your goal: you want to win in the confrontation. In order to do that you must have supporting information available to you. So look for that kind of supportive information! Concentrate and focus your search.

It's possible to skim quickly through a vast amount of printed material if you identify key words or phrases that will lead you to appropriate data and which will be pertinent to your confrontation. With a bit of practice in this technique you'll find that useful data will almost jump off the pages at you.

Record the Specifics

The next step is to record the specifics in the notes you will be using during the confrontation. It will do you no good to find the information if you can't use it when it counts. It's usually a good practice to be over–prepared with such supportive material. Better to have more than you need than to come up lacking.

Don't feel compelled to use everything you find. Don't force every citation into the presentation. If you were to try to do that, you could end up by making a dire mistake. You could become so concerned with trying to find a place for every piece of evidence that you lose track of the flow of ideas. If that were to happen, you would have no good idea of where, when, and what to use to support your position.

Knowing What *Not* To Use

Know exactly what supportive data you have, and pull it out only when it fits. Certainly, you can direct the conversation toward a point where a specific citation will provide strong support, but be selective.

Don't fire all of your big guns too quickly either. Let the flow of information develop so that when you do use a citation it will carry power. You don't want to shoot the arrow into the air; you want to hit a target!

Winging It—Without Supporting Material

What if you can't find appropriate citations? What if you don't have the time or the resources to conduct that preliminary research? Is there anything else to do to strengthen your position and avoid having to say "I think that . . . "?

There are a couple of techniques you can use in such a situation. Whenever possible, remember to avoid using the word "I" because it provides an easy opportunity for your opponent to counter with a purely personal opinion. Another personal opinion is as good as yours, so you don't have any advantage. That situation becomes a stand-off.

Rather than using "I", refer to something outside of yourself. Use a reference that will seem to give strength to your position. An "outside" piece of evidence will make you sound like you're on more solid ground. In the grammatical sense, use the third person to state your evidence or to support your position.

Employ such phrases as "There is a belief that . . . ," or "It has been demonstrated that . . . ," or "A review shows that . . . " None of these is really evidence, but each sounds stronger than just saying, "I think . . . ." Be cautious with this tactic, however, because if your opponents are alert, they won't let you get away with such an unsupported statement. They just might ask, "What review?," "Who demonstrated?," or "Who believes?"

This can, therefore, be a calculated risk each time you use it, so employ it with care. Of course, you are always far better off and on safer ground if you have a legitimate, identified citation. You may have only one opportunity at this confrontation so make the best of it, and take the time to prepare, if it is at all humanly possible to work it into your schedule.

If you are caught by surprise, and you feel the need to strengthen your position beyond a simple "I think . . . " use a phrase many academics find useful. If you were to listen in on a faculty meeting or academic discussion you won't hear "I think . . . ," but rather you will hear, "I would argue that . . . "

Doesn't that sound stronger–and perhaps even well informed?

In academia and in debating circles people "argue" in favor of or in opposition to a particular position. The phrase "I would argue that . . . " seems to indicate that careful consideration has been given to all elements of a situation, and only after such deliberate consideration has a conclusion been reached. There seems to be strength in the statement because "argue" suggests a powerful action. There is the sound of conviction! "I think . . . ," on the other hand, can sound tired, weak, and cautious.

"I would argue that . . . " is still only a personal opinion, but by using it you won't get trapped into giving a specific citation; yet it will put you in a stronger position in the eyes of your opponent during the confrontation. It will serve you well in the brief moment that you need it.

It is also a phrase that is not in common use in many circles so the surprise element will also be working in your favor during the meeting.

You want to win, so use every element of strength you can. Using the elements of surprise and the perception of focussed research can be of great value.

6

Working with Other, Miscellaneous Factors

WRITING THAT WILL BE READ

Most of our concerns so far have concentrated on oral exchanges, one person talking to another person. We have examined both face-to-face confrontation, and confrontation at a distance through the telephone. We've looked at places and conditions affecting the outcome of communication and at the mechanisms that can be applied in spoken exchanges.

Although most confrontations are oral, we would be remiss if we didn't look at selected techniques involving writing.

We're referring to writing that goes far beyond the note–taking we discussed in another section of this book. You'll recall that we suggested how notes could be used for a number of reasons and a variety of purposes. They provide an accurate record of our pre-meeting research; they enable us to punctuate our presentations; they allow us to buy time during a confrontation when we refer to them; and they serve as an excellent method of breaking our opponents' train of thought by deliberately asking them to repeat a comment so that we can write it accurately.

Note–taking, then is an important skill to apply prior to and during the confrontation, but sometimes the written word itself will constitute the entire confrontation.

Sometimes our communication will be through the written word alone. It is that use we'll be looking at here.

Written Information vs. Oral Information

First, what are the differences between providing information in writing and providing it in oral form?

Other than the obvious, the major difference is in the method and the time frame in which we get "feedback" from our adversary.

Feedback is the method by which we assess the effectiveness with which we are communicating our thoughts. In an oral exchange we get instant feedback. Tone of voice on the telephone, pitch, pace, etc. let us know something about how our message is being received.

In face-to-face confrontation these factors certainly are observable, and we can also see changes in facial expression, body positions, gestures, etc.

The key difference is in the feedback. The feedback comes in oral communication while we are expressing our thoughts and ideas. We can tell continually how well, or how poorly, we are doing.

With written confrontation, however, that immediacy of response is gone. We can't get instant feedback so we must give even more attention to the message construction than would otherwise be necessary.

The Process

In order to prepare a written confrontation, you must still work in advance to identify the significant elements which define your adversary. Even though you will be writing rather than speaking, the same cultural, emotional, and social factors which shaped a receiver's reaction in person are in operation when the person is reading. The opponent is still the same person, subject to the same pressures.

In order to be most effective, therefore, you must attempt to construct your written message in such a way that your position will prevail even at a distance and separated by time. How do you do that?

First of all, picture the reader.

Who is the person?

Where is the person likely to be when reading your material?

What might the surroundings be like?

When will it be read? Before/after a big meeting? At the office? At home?

Will the material constitute an "unusual" request/demand?

Will it be a "major problem" to be resolved?

What does the person look like?

Next, think about your relationship to the reader.

Will the reader recognize your name right away?

Will your request/demand come "out of the blue," or have you been in contact before?

Are you business "equals"?

Can you force the reader to do something, or must you ask for her or his cooperation?

Is the reader likely to be the deciding party, or will you have to go through her or him to get to the real decision maker?

Once you have thought through these items it's time to write down what you want. What will be included in the letter?

What do you want the reader to do?

What will you do?

What led up to this letter?

What research have you done?

What time table is requested?

Who else might be involved?

What are the next steps?

After you have made these notes and others that will be appropriate for your specific issue, organize them in the way that will have the greatest impact.

What *must* be included?

What *can be omitted?*

What should come first? Next? Last?

Finally, how should the letter "sound"? What emotional feeling should be communicated?

Are you angry? Hurt? Defensive?

Are you requesting action or demanding it?

Are you entitled to get what you are asking for, or are you seeking some special consideration?

Is this a "bother" for you because of the reader's incompetence, or are you excited by this?

If you don't go through this exercise prior to constructing your written message you are running a risk.

Remember, instant feedback is impossible, but there will be feedback. You must execute the message in the way that will maximize your chances of winning.

These three sets of questions will help you to organize by focusing on three critical elements:

1. The specific characteristics of your opponent,

2. The elements of your relationship,

3. The "tone" which will be most appropriate.

This careful advanced planning will result in a written communication which will serve you well.

Now write the letter! Then, put it aside for a while. Finally, re-read it.

Does the letter communicate *exactly* what you want, in the way you want? Or does it somehow miss the mark? If so, re-write it. All too often in our haste to get something into the mail we don't do this critical review and revision. We sacrifice accuracy and power for speed.

The purpose of the communication is to be successful; the purpose is not to win a race. Even if your purpose were to write something very quickly, once it goes into the mailbox the speed is out of your hands. A self-imposed delay early in the process can save a great deal of time in the long run because you will not have to clarify, or expand, or provide additional material, or revise in some other way after an unfavorable response.

If and when you are tempted to write and send something quickly, and therefore skip one or more of these steps, let me share a quote I saw many years ago:

> It is foolish to believe there just isn't enough time to do a job right in the first place when there is always enough time to do it over again!

Your written work must be done correctly in the first place, and then you won't have to do it over again.

THE PEN IS MIGHTIER
THAN THE SWORD

It's appropriate at this point to spend a little time thinking about this confrontation business from another aspect.

What we're really concerned about is *communication;* and there are a few specific elements that we should cover. Whole volumes have been written about the communication process so we won't try to duplicate that extensive material here, but we should consider some of the basic factors associated with the process.

A Continuous Process

First of all, communication is a process, so it should be considered as on-going. It doesn't have a specific beginning or ending; it is continuous, and we can elect any one of a number of places to begin a discussion.

For our purposes let us assume that there are two people meeting face to face. Our example, therefore, fits the confrontation meeting conditions we have stressed so far.

Common Experience for Common Understanding

Communication is the process by which an idea in the mind of one participant is transferred to the mind of the other participant. In order to carry out this transfer some mechanism is needed. The mechanism might be words, gestures, pictures, songs, paintings, or any of a variety of other options. The significant factor in selecting the mechanism is that both parties must understand the mechanism. A person blind from birth cannot understand what "blue" means in the same way a sighted person does. A word spoken in French means nothing to someone unfamiliar with that language. *Remember, without common experience there cannot be common understanding.*

When you are planning to engage in any kind of communication (and this is specially important in a confrontation) be sure to select and use techniques that are meaningful to your opponent as well as to yourself.

Because communication means the exchange of thoughts and ideas, *what your opponent thinks you mean is far more important than what you know you mean.* Consider this for a moment. You already know something, so the confrontation isn't required in order for you to gain that information. *The confrontation is required in order for you to get your opponent to think the way you do, to agree with you.*

What Motivates Your Opponent?

Therefore, you must select and employ mechanisms that are important to your opponent. When you construct your messages, begin by considering the receiver's needs, expectations, requirements, etc. What makes your opponent "tick"? What will be important enough to your opponent to convince that person to do what you want done?

That importance might be anything from avoiding a bigger problem, to getting a promotion, to getting you out of her or his hair, to being of genuine assistance to you. Try to get to know something about your opponent in order to use that information to help establish your position.

When we consider the basic elements of the communication process and communication theory we can see the application of the specific recommendations made earlier in this book: for example, name-dropping, costumes, and other tactics which reflect how knowledge of the receiver will enable you to construct effective messages and apply winning strategies.

Your Mission

Your mission is to convince your opponent to agree with your thoughts. You want that person to reach the same conclusion you have reached about what constitutes an acceptable resolution of an issue.

How To Know When You Have Won

In order to assure that you "win," however, you must be sure of what will *signal* the win. You must know exactly what you want and what you can expect before the confrontation takes place, in order to know when you have achieved it.

Tell yourself what the winning factors will be.

What are the expected outcomes?

What are the desired outcomes?

What is your point of view?

What is your adversary's point of view?

When will you know that you have won?

Let's put this another way. *If you don't know exactly what you want, you won't know when you have it!*

In addition, if you don't know the strengths and weaknesses of your opponent it will be impossible to plan carefully a course of action. You may win, but then again you may not. That's a risky way to enter into the confrontation.

Select, Select, Select

Finally, if you know what communication mechanisms, are available you'll be able to select what will give you the greatest leverage. Select the words, gestures, postures, etc. that will support your positions.

The key word is *select.* This is an action oriented concept. If you simply let things happen and "let nature take its course," you reduce your chances of winning. And losing makes no sense. The trick is to *increase the chances for success by knowing and applying the variety of skills and techniques available to you, when you select and arrange the elements of your confrontation.*

Even though those same skills are available to your opponent too, if you prepare your position knowing what the other person might do, you can still win, by planning ahead and selecting your actions carefully.

7
Coming To Closure

DRAFTING RIGHTS:
WHO SAYS WHAT AND WHEN

A successful confrontation, either oral or written, does not always conclude with a clear win or with all details and issues fully resolved. Sometimes the appropriate conclusion of a confrontation is an agreement to meet again.

Time pressures, data collection, or logistics could necessitate another meeting prior to resolution and closure.

If that happens to you, take the initiative concerning the next steps. Don't simply agree to meet again at an appointed time and place, but set an agenda!

Write down what you will do at the next meeting. Get your adversary to agree to the items on the agenda that you write. This is a variation of the note-taking technique in which you "play back" words to your opponent. If you can use the opponent's own words so much the better.

If, at the end of your meeting, there is still a difference of opinion concerning the eventual resolution you can often move closer to achieving your position at the subsequent meeting by volunteering to "summarize the discussion so far and the direction it seems to be taking."

Your opponent will usually welcome that suggestion.

The opponent usually doesn't want to do it, but feels it's a good way to get the thoughts down on paper.

If the present meeting has progressed far enough to justify this action, you might even volunteer to "draft the mutually agreeable resolution we seem to be reaching. We can then solve the problem at hand." Lawyers call this "taking drafting rights." Although this means a little more work for you it gives you a tremendous advantage at this state of the confrontation.

You get to state the conditions, agreements, recommendations, and resolutions in the words you select. Further, this technique often allows you to get what you want just by writing it down!

Often your opponents will agree with your general overview and total summation even though they might not have gone quite as far or given quite as much on a particular point if they had summarized the meeting themselves. And that's the whole point!

When you have such drafting rights you have the opportunity to write exactly what you want—the way you want it. Your opponents must then be careful and thorough enough to remove any items they don't agree with. If they happen to miss something, that point remains one for you.

Therefore, even though you might be tempted to take the easy way out and let your opponents write such a summary and set of recommendations, resist that temptation. You do it!

Take the time and care to present your case. Use the notes you took during the meeting, and wherever possible, incorporate direct quotes made by your opponents.

They will recognize their own words in the document, and that recognition will usually set up a positive reaction in them. They will see that you are being reasonable, thorough, and careful. Clearly, you will be demonstrating your own desire to be fair and accurate.

That perception on the opponents' part (whether accurate or not) will make it a little more difficult for them to spot all the items which they might otherwise take out of the document. And, once again, if they don't take something out, it's there for you. You win.

Drafting rights will always work to your advantage if you have them. If, on the other hand, your opponents write the draft, be very cautious. Look for anything that might present the most remote possibility of a problem, and omit it.

As a rule of thumb, if you don't agree completely with a statement, get rid of it. Take your time. Be very careful to review all points, project how you will handle them at the next meeting, and agree to the agenda when...*you* are ready.

8

Synthesis and Conclusion

WHAT DOES ALL OF THIS MEAN?

Every day we encounter situations that require us to compete with others. The competition might be gentle and rather unimportant, or the outcome might have a significant influence on our lives. In either case, competition exists, and we should try to win as often as possible.

Under no circumstances can all of us win all the time. Obviously, that would be an impossibility, but, we should work to earn a good "batting average." We should plan and execute actions designed to produce winning outcomes. And remember that that never just happens accidentally!

Certainly winning requires work, but first it requires the formation and acceptance of an attitude on your part. You must recognize your own strengths and limitations. You must build on those strengths and not waste time and effort being upset by the limitations. You must believe that you can—and will—win. Everyone has limitations, so you're not different. The difference can be in how you deal with them.

Often, of course, it is possible to work out solutions to conflicts in which both sides will win. Your first goal is to win—if you can help your opponent win also, so much the better.

103

A careful, honest examination right now will start you on the path that will help assure you of success in future confrontations. You'll know without question what you have to work with.

When you see a confrontation coming you can then concentrate on your opponent. That assessment will enable you to plan how to use most effectively what you have at your disposal.

What does all of this mean? Simply stated, it means you have to:

1. Know what you can do,

2. Know what you want to do,

3. Structure the situation so you get what you want.

Develop the confidence to realize that, indeed, you can make things happen your way. You can be a doer; you don't have to be a victim.

THE CONCEPT OF COMPETITION

One final word on the concept of competition. Competition doesn't always mean right against wrong. It often refers to the desire for one good idea to triumph over another good idea. The difference is in the perception, and you want your perception to be the accepted one. If the other good idea wins, well that's how it goes. You just didn't have enough information or power to win that time. But, another time always exists.

Approach

From now on, take a direct interest in how you approach competitive situations. Examine your adversary as far in advance as possible, and, as much as you possibly can, manipulate the physical conditions in which the confrontation will take place.

Watch for openings and look at the behavior of others.

Think about what you want to accomplish.

Ian how you can use all of the personal and environmental factors to your advantage.

Act according to your plan.

Judge the effectiveness of your actions.

Revise your actions if the outcome was not what you expected—and try again.

One Last Word of Caution

In every case these same tactics can be used by your opponent, so learn them well. Practice, and use them well, and beware when they are being used on you. If your opponents use these tactics, you will know what they are up to. Because you know the rules, you can counter move, quickly and efficiently. You won't be fooled or overpowered. Don't let yourself be manipulated or controlled by these mechanisms and tactics.

Finally, be sure to pick the right time and the right tactic for you, so you will . . .

Never Kick a Kangaroo!!!

9

Epilogue

SETTING PRIORITIES

We've covered a great deal of territory and many specific factors related to dealing with confrontations. We have focused on a variety of elements—Physical, Emotional, Social—and several related factors including organizational and writing skills.

We have had the luxury of addressing each of these as separate and discrete; but we all know that, in the "real world" no such luxury exists. The Physical, Emotional, and Social elements are all interrelated, and we have to deal with these multiple factors all the time—at the same time. So, we have to set up some priorities in order to ready ourselves for the confrontation.

In this final section, therefore, we'll walk through the process by using a check list/laundry list/outline based on the simple idea of "First things first." We'll cover the steps but not try to repeat all of the material all over again.

The priorities are set by the sequence of events we must follow; as we have said often, you must know what you want. That's step one!

But, be careful. There is an old adage which states, "Be careful what you ask for—you just might get it!"

REQUIREMENTS AND EXPECTATIONS

Think through your requirements and expectations, and phrase them carefully and clearly so you know what you want, and so your adversary knows what you want. Through your statement or inquiry, you set the tone and the parameters within which your adversary will respond.

There are many ways to approach this statement of requirements or expectations so pick what is most appropriate—and beneficial—for you. The major options available include:

- Give an order. (Do this . . .)

- Provide a direction. (Please submit by . . .)

- Make a request. (Will you . . .)

- Provide conditions. (If possible, will you . . .)

The opening sentence you select will determine the subsequent course of action for the confrontation; so select it carefully.

Remember, you'll get results in proportion to what you expect. Make sure your expectations are clear to all parties—both you and your adversary.

A PROCESS CHECKLIST

Now, let's walk through the process using the six directives: Watch, Think, Plan, Act, Judge, Revise. Use the spaces as work space. Jot down items, thoughts, questions, etc. to supplement what is provided. This listing should be considered as a general working document that can be modified to fit any specific situation. Some items will be expanded or reduced in relation to discrete topics, but most of them will be appropriate most of the time.

Let's walk through the items.

Watch

Look for openings, and observe the behavior of your adversary.

* Is the "problem" or topic of the confrontation a sudden surprise?

  _____

* When did it start?_____
* How did it start?_____
* Who caused it?_____
* Was it deliberate or accidental?_____
* It is just a misunderstanding?_____
* Is it a serious difference?_____
* It is likely to have long term effects on you?_____
* Who are the "players"?_____
* Who is your adversary?_____
* What do you know about your adversary?

  Position in the organization_____

  Power_____

  Status_____

  Influence_____

* What kind of person is your adversary?

  Dictatorial_____

  Sympathetic_____

  Open Minded_____

  Tough_____

  Understanding_____

  Anxious to help_____

  "By-the-book"_____

Notes:

_____

_____

_____

_____

_____

Think

What do you want to accomplish?

- What do you need to "win?"

    Immediate action?_____

    Long term behavior change?_____

    Change of operation?_____

    Small variation in a process?_____

    One-time action or reaction?_____

- What does your adversary need to "win"?

    Beat you down?_____

    Immediate action?_____

    Long term behavior change?_____

    Slight change in your position?_____

    One-time accommodation?_____

- Can you afford to provide that win?_____
- How soon do you want action?_____
- How do you expect the "win" to be demonstrated?_____
- Can you afford to hold out until you get exactly what you want?

_____

- What will you accept?_____

- What are you willing to give up?_____
- What is most important to you?_____
- What do you *need* as opposed to what do you *want?*_____
- Are you willing to negotiate with your current adversary to get a resolution?_____
- Will you—should you—demand to meet with someone at a higher level?_____
- Who? How high?_____
- What will be your justification for such a demand?_____
- What can you find out about that person before demanding such a subsequent meeting?_____
- Is that person more or less likely to see things your way?____
- Why do you think so?_____

Notes:

_____

_____

_____

_____

_____

Plan

How can you use the personal and environmental factors to your advantage?

- What must you do to get ready for the confrontation?

Research_____

Evaluate the "turf"_____

- Should you meet at an office?

  Whose?_____

  Why?_____

- What do you know about your adversary's "turf"?_____

- Should you meet on neutral territory?

  Whose?_____

  What kind of place?_____

  　　Restaurant?_____

  　　Friend's office, home, etc.?_____

- What kind of setting will be best and most practical for you?

  Business?_____

  Social?_____

  Why?_____

- How can you "set up" the confrontation in your favor?

  Phone call suggesting time and place?_____

  Letter suggesting time and place?_____

- Where/How can you get the data you need?

  Personal experience?_____

  Correspondence?_____

  Library search?_____

  Corporate/Institutional publications?_____

  Other personal contacts?_____

  　　Business?_____

  　　Social?_____

- Who can tell you about your adversary?

  Receptionist?_____

  Secretary?_____

  Colleagues?_____

  Public Information Staff?_____

  Other?_____

- Where can you get background on your adversary's organization?

  Personal visitation?_____

  Newspapers?_____

  Corporate newsletters?_____

  Library?_____

  Public Relations department?_____

  Other?_____

- What data will you need?

  Statistics?_____

  Photo copies of documents?_____

  Depositions?_____

  Institutional policies?_____

  Laws?_____

  Other?_____

- Where can you get that information?_____

- How long will it take?_____

- What will it cost?_____

- What options do you have if some elements are unavailable?

  _____

- How should you look?_____

    Clothing?_____

    "Props" (Brief case, etc.)?_____

    Other?_____

- How *do* you look?_____

- How do you sound?_____

- When, where, and with whom can you rehearse?_____

- Do you know enough appropriate jargon?_____

- How, where can you learn more if necessary?_____

Notes:

_____

_____

_____

_____

_____

Act

Follow your plan. Do your homework early. Carry out all of the elements of your plan and then ask:

- What will you do *first* when you meet your adversary?_____

- How will you do it?_____

- What action will you expect from your opponent?_____

- How will you respond?_____
- What is your position?_____
- What is the background?_____
- What are your expectations?_____
- When must your expectations be met?_____
- How can you avoid losing your composure?_____
- What information will you need to record in notes?_____
- When will it be advantageous to play back quotes from your opponent's comments which support your position?_____
- How will you push for closure as soon as arguments have been presented by both sides?_____
- When should you volunteer to "draft" the agreement—if it is necessary and appropriate?_____
- How will you arrange another meeting if you can't get agreement?_____

  What others, if any, should attend?_____

  When should the meeting take place?_____

- What will your agenda be for that meeting?_____

Notes:

_____

_____

_____

_____

_____

_____

Judge

Did it work? Finally, when the meeting is over, and you are alone consider the following:

• Did you get what you wanted?

Exactly?_____

"Sort of"_____

Not Yet!_____

Nope!_____

• Why were you successful?

Good planning?_____

Good homework?_____

Fast thinking?_____

Strong evidence?_____

Just lucky?_____

Other?_____

• Why did you fail?

Poor planning?_____

Poor homework?_____

Dull responses?_____

Inappropriate data?_____

Opponent was lucky?_____

Other?_____

• How can you avoid those problems next time?_____

• How can you find out more about your opponent, the "turf,"

and the options?_____

- What skills should you develop to improve your performance?

  Speaking?_____

  Writing?_____

  Data Collection?_____

  Dress?_____

  Other?_____

Notes:

_____

_____

_____

_____

_____

Revise

Review your progress and plan ahead for next time. If necessary—make changes.

- What will you do differently next time?

  Homework?_____

  Data collection?_____

  "Props"?_____

  "Turf"?_____

  "Jargon"?_____

  Other?_____

- How can you clarify your explanation of what you want/expect/need?_____

- Where can you get assistance in developing your skills?

  Classes?_____

  Private tutoring?_____

  Reading?_____

  Practice what you already know?_____

  Other?_____

Go back to the very beginning, and start all over again. Ask yourself some *hard* questions including:

- Did I really prepare?

  Do the necessary research?_____

  Study my opponent?_____

  Carefully prepare my position/argument?_____

  Listen to my opponent and respond appropriately to

  positions contrary to mine?_____

  Take good notes?_____

  Know *exactly* what I wanted?_____

  Make that clear to my opponent?_____

- Did I give in before I had to?_____

  How can I prevent that next time?_____

Notes:

_____

_____

_____

_____

_____

REVIEW, AND BE GOOD
TO YOURSELF

A careful—and honest review of all of these items will help you form an accurate picture of the entire confrontation process. You'll be able to tell where your strengths lie and where you need work.

You'll be able to establish priorities related to what you have to do to become successful in these confrontations. We mentioned "batting averages" earlier when we indicated that you won't win every confrontation: don't expect to; and don't drive yourself crazy when you lose.

A caution: never enter into a confrontation with the idea that you *may* lose. Think "win," and act like a winner at all times.

Always concentrate on your strengths and focus them on your opponent's weaknesses. Through observation and advanced planning, figure out just what those weaknesses are before the confrontation begins.

Now we all know that extremely significant and highly important confrontations don't enter our lives every day—and for that we are all grateful! But we need to sharpen and hone our skills in advance so we are ready when action is required.

How can we do that? Simple! Practice!

Practice On Your Friends

Use your friends and colleagues for this practice. If you enlist the support of friends it's easy to set up role-play situations. Pick a problem—real or imagined—that you plan to address and have your friend play the part of the adversary. Provide your opponent with as much information as you can. Without such information, your "adversary" (friend) won't be of much help to you. You'll win too easily, and you won't get much practice for the "real thing" when it comes along. Of course this technique requires a willingness on the part of your friend to participate in this role-playing. Some friends are quite willing, but others might think of it as just play and not be very interested. In either case, the factors that start the role-playing cause the results to be artificial, and therefore, lacking in the realism you might want to test and strengthen your skills.

So try practicing your skills with a friend who is totally unaware of what you are doing. Create an adversary simply by taking a position which is contrary to one you know a friend holds on a topic of interest (business, sports, travel, etc.). You might try something like this.

- Pick out a friend who is to be the "adversary," but keep that fact to yourself.

- Select a topic about which you know your adversary has a firm position. (for example: "Brand X car is the best car on the road."

- Develop your position. (Brand X is poorly designed and has low value.)

- Work through the Watch, Think, Plan steps described earlier. Do your homework on the topic.

- Pick a time and a place to engage your "adversary" in a discussion about cars.

- Act out your plan, and do whatever you can to convince your "adversary" that you are right.

- Use all of the skills at your command.

- Judge if you are successful. If so, good. If not——

- In the quiet of your room, review your actions and plan for the next time.

In addition to this being good practice for you, it also livens up luncheons, cocktail parties, and long car rides.

Don't get too "pushy" though, or you might find yourself doing monologues more often that you might like!

PLANNING AHEAD

Because we live in a complex society, conflicts and confrontations—large and small—will engulf us every day. None of us wants to react all the time; we all want to be winners and to control what happens to us. The tactics, techniques, and control mechanisms we have at our disposal will truly enable us to successfully compete in these social, economic, legal, and other confrontations.

Just plan ahead. Use your strengths against your opponent's weaknesses. Don't let yourself get into a contest that you can't win. If for some strange reason you had to compete with a kangaroo you would be well aware that it can kick a lot better than you can. So pick a different type of conflict. This little analogy reflects the caution described through this book. Remember it when you prepare to select your terms for a confrontation. Choose your strongest characteristics to use against your opponent's weakest ones, so you will *never kick a kangaroo*.

Appendix A

Suggested Readings

We've covered a great deal of material, but there is certainly much more we can learn about personal interaction, confrontations, and control mechanisms. The following books will provide a varied sampling of what is available. Some are quite serious; some are great fun. All of these provide much good and useful information. Happy reading.

Are Your Lights On?, Donald C. Gauge, Gerald M. Weinberg; Ethnotech, Inc., 1976.

Art of Getting Your Own Sweet Way (The), Philip B. Crosby; McGraw-Hill Book Co., 1972.

Art of Negotiating (The), Gerrald I. Nierenberg; Hawthorne Books, 1968.

Assertive Option (The), Patricia Jakubowski, Arthur J. Lang; Research Press Co., 1978.

Body Language of Sex, Power, and Aggression (The), M. Evans & Co., 1977.

Body Politics, Nancy M. Henley; Prentice Hall, 1977.

Communicate, C. Parkinson, Rowe Nigel; Prentice Hall International, 1978.

Coping With Difficult People, Robert M. Bramson, Ph.D; Anchor Press/ Doubleday, 1981.

C Zone (The), Robert Kriegel, Ph.D, Marilyn Harris Krieger, Ph.D; Anchor Press/Doubleday, 1984.

Don't Shoot the Dog, Karen Pryor, Simon and Schuster, 1984.

59 Second Employee (The): How to stay ahead of Your 1 Minute Manager, Rae André, Ph.D, Peter D. Ward, J. D.; Houghton Mifflin Co., 1984.

Gestures, Desmond Morris, Peter Collett, Peter Marsh, Marie O'Shaughnessy; Stein and Day, 1979.

Go For It!, Irene C. Kassarla; Delacorte Press, 1984.

How to Read a Person Like a Book: and what to do about it, Gerald I. Nierenberg, Henry H. Calero; Cornerstone Library, 1981.

How To Sell Yourself, Joe Girard, Robert Casemore; Simon and Schuster, 1979.

Human Relations in Business, Fred J. Carvell; Macmillan Co., 1970.

Jobmanship: How to get ahead by "psyching out" your boss and co-workers, S. R. Redford; Macmillan Publishing Co., 1978.

Language of Body (The), Alexander Lowen, MD; Collier Books, 1958.

Live For Success, John T. Molloy; William Morrow & Co., 1981.

"Mac" Conversations About Management, Elliott Carlisle; McGraw-Hill Book Co., 1983.

Managing Through Insight, Charles D. Flory, Editor; World Publishing Co., 1968.

Nonverbal Communication for Business Success, Ken Cooper; Amacom, 1979.

People Specialists (The), Stanley M. Herman; Alfred Knopf, 1968.

Psycho-Cybernetics & Self-fulfillment, Maxwell Maltz; Bantam Books, 1970.

Put Offs—Come Ons, Psychological Maneuvers and Strategems, A. M. Chapman, MD; G. P. Putnam's Sons, 1968.

Secrets of Getting Results Through People (The), A. Gordon Bradt; Parker Publishing Co., 1967.

3 Boxes of Life (The), Richard N. Bolles; Ten Speed Press, 1978.

Winning by Negotiation, Tessa Albert Warschaw; McGraw-Hill, 1980.

Winning Images, Robert L. Shook; Macmillan Publishing Co., 1977.

Work Ethic (The), David J. Cherrington; Amacom, 1980.

You Can Negotiate Anything, Herb Cohen; Lyle Stuart, Inc., 1980.

Appendix B

For Practice

The following pages contain brief descriptions of various confrontational situations in which you might find yourself from time to time.

Each scenario is followed by a series of questions/comments which should serve as a check list to help you prepare for such a confrontation.

The material is included here for practice and to provide assistance in reviewing details covered in the key sections of the book.

Working with the Physical Factors

- Movement
- Eye Contact
- Costume
- Sex
- Territory
- Props

Working with the Emotional Factors

- "Can do" attitude
- Pick the Contact
- Affect the Balance

Working with the Social Factors

- Vocabulary
- Name Dropping
- Jargon
- Citations

As with the other sections you are encouraged to add items of your own to the check list.

You will have to assess your own strengths and weaknesses as you go through the exercises. You have to consider such factors as your own sex, size, voice, experience, what kind of clothing would be appropriate, and what props you could use to your advantage.

You'll have to determine just how strong your own "can do" attitude is and how strongly you can assert yourself in order to achieve success. Every one of us is different, and we will react differently in these situations. This practice will give you a "leg up" on determining how you can best present yourself to win when the confrontation is a real one.

Picture the places where the confrontations might have taken place—places that are like the places you have visited. You know your immediate surroundings far better than anyone else does. Where would be the best place for the confrontation? What would you need to win? Try to personalize the situations as much as possible in order to make them most useful to you.

Finally, given the specifics you add to the following general situations, what vocabulary would be most productive for you? Is a "special" vocabulary needed?

Who do you know that might be helpful in the situation?

Do you know the laws, policies, etc. that relate to this situation? Can you find them? Where?

These exercises will be most helpful if you personalize the situations following the patterns contained in this book. We have covered a great many general situations and conditions; now is your chance to put them into practice. Get ready to use them as they fit you. Have fun!

SITUATION NO. 1:

You are on vacation with a tour group, and you win a "free dinner for two" at the hotel restaurant. All your meals have been paid for already, however, so the prize as it stands doesn't really provide anything. You want to win some kind of exchange that will benefit you.

Reaction/Action:

How do you get what you want?

- Just ask for cash instead.

- Tell the manager to credit your account to cover items not included in the price of the trip.

- Order wine with dinner until the amount equal to the dinners has been reached.

- Tell your tour guide to "take care" of it for you.

- Ask the hotel manager what you can do.

- Say "thank you" for the prize, and then simply tell the manager that you assume the dollar amount will be credited to your account.

- Say "thank you" and take the prize. Usually there is a card or token identifying the actual prize value. Say nothing else—yet!

- At check out time when you "settle up" the bill for any extras simply present the token and deduct the amount from the bill yourself when you make the final payment.

- Other_____

_____

_____

_____

_____

Analysis:

- Which option is the best one for you?_____

  _____

- What tactics or strategies would you use?_____

  _____

- What actions would you take?_____

  _____

- Why?_____

  _____

SITUATION NO. 2:

On a business trip you arrive late at your hotel and discover that your reservation has been cancelled by someone. After much discussion with the reservations clerk you learn that the only space available is an "executive suite" for which the nightly rate is twice what you had been quoted for the cancelled room.

Reaction/Action:

How do you get what you want?

- Go to another hotel—if they have rooms available.
- Pay the higher price for the executive suite.
- Demand to know why the reservation was cancelled and to be given your room.
- Call for the manager, and make the demands of him.
- Ask the clerk, or manager, if you can have the suite for the price of the room.
- Inform the clerk—or manager—that you will take the suite, but that you expect to pay the rate for the less–expensive room.
- Rather than propose ideas and solutions, just ask the manager how he plans to settle this entire matter. Wait to see what he suggests. It may turn out to be a "non-problem."
- Call the Better Business Bureau.
- Write a letter of complaint to the president of the hotel. (This won't do any good right away, but it could help in the future.)
- Take the suite. Refuse to pay the high rate at check out time.
- Other_____

_____

_____

_____

_____

Analysis:

- Which option is the best one for you?_____

  _____

- What tactics or strategies would you use?_____

  _____

- What actions would you take?_____

  _____

- Why?_____

  _____

SITUATION NO. 3:

You go to the "fast printing" place to pick up an order of new stationery for your office and find it is not satisfactory. The printing is just "slightly off-center," and it bothers you a bit. The printer thinks it's okay. You are dissatisfied.

Reaction/Action:

How do you get what you want?

- Pay. Take the order. Never go back.
- Tell the printer you won't do business with her again if she doesn't correct the order.
- Insist that the entire order be re-printed—at no cost to you.
- Agree with the printer's demand that you pay for the extra paper for the re-print, as long as you are not charged for the additional labor.
- Write a check for the order. Take the material. Call the bank to stop the check. Then call the printer. Tell her what you did.
- Demand to see the "quality assurance/guarantee" statement that most such businesses have. Read it, and quote an appropriate section to the manager, if you can find such a section.
- If there isn't such a section, question why any such service business doesn't stand behind the quality of its work.
- Ask the manager if her general policy is to ignore the concerns of her customers. (Do these things in a location and in a loud enough voice to allow other customers to hear you.)
- If the job won't be redone ask how much the manager plans to discount your order because of the "inferior quality" of the work. (You need

something to use right away so you will take the poor-quality material, but you'll have to have the work re-done by a reputable company.

- Never go back.

- Other_____

_____

_____

_____

_____

Analysis:

- Which option is the best one for you?_____

_____

- What tactics or strategies would you use?_____

_____

- What actions would you take?_____

_____

- Why?_____

_____

SITUATION NO. 4:

You want to get a flight at a time earlier than the one for which you purchased a ticket at a special reduced fare. The agent tells you that there is space on the plane, but it will cost you more because "all the special fare" seats have been sold.

Reaction/Action:

How do you get what you want?

- Pay the extra fare.
- Wait for the later plane.
- Ask to see the supervisor.
- Request an updated count of the "special fare" seats.
- Become annoyed; talk loud; demand to know why you aren't being allowed to take one of the seats which will remain empty for the entire flight whether or not you are on the plane.
- Ask at the gate to be put on the "Stand by" list. (If there are seats available, you'll get on, at no extra cost.)
- Ask the agent why they didn't tell you about the stand-by arrangement in the first place, and avoid all the problems.
- Other_____

_____

_____

_____

_____

Analysis:

- What option is the best one for you?_____

_____

- What tactics or strategies would you use?_____

    _____

- What actions would you take?_____

    _____

- Why?_____

    _____

    _____

    _____

    _____

    _____

    _____

SITUATION NO. 5:

You have been at a new job for only two weeks, "low man on the totem pole." You overhear your manager telling a co-worker that he needs to assign someone to a new task. You don't know how to perform that new task, but you do know that doing it could lead to an eventual promotion.

Reaction/Action:

How do you get what you want?

- Forget it! You can't do the job anyway so why worry about it?

- Sign up for a management training program and/or a college course covering the subject so you'll be ready the next time such an opportunity comes along.

- Ask one of your fellow workers to suggest to your manager that you might be a possible choice, to "put in a good word" for you even though you are not yet able to perform the required task.

- Tell your manager what you overheard and that you "can do" that job—even if you can't.

- Volunteer for the assignment, and if you get it then do all you can as fast as you can to learn how to do it. (First say "Yes, I can." and then find out how later.)

- Other_____

_____

_____

_____

_____

Analysis:

- Which option is the best for you?_____

  _____

- What tactics or strategies would you use?_____

  _____

- What actions would you take?_____

  _____

- Why?_____

  _____

  _____

  _____

  _____

SITUATION NO. 6:

At your place of work there are many things you would like to do, but you are not getting the opportunity to do them. You would rather not do some of the menial things that you are doing now.

Reaction/Action:

How do you get what you want?

- Keep plugging along. Someday your faithful service will be recognized and rewarded.
- Complain to fellow workers that you are being wasted.
- Write a letter to personnel.
- Tell your manager that you want other things to do, to give your menial tasks to someone else.
- Let everyone know that you are looking for a job at another company where they will "appreciate all you can do for them."
- Start sending résumés to places listed in the "positions available" or "help wanted" section of the Sunday business section of the local newspaper.
- Sulk. Goof off.
- Complete preliminary work on a project you would like to do. Show it to your manager and say, "I'd like to develop this further if it's O.K. with you." (Show her what you can do, and ask for the chance to do it.)
- Other_____

_____

_____

_____

_____

Analysis:

- Which option is best for you?_____

  _____

- What tactics or strategies would you use?_____

  _____

- What actions would you take?_____

  _____

- Why?_____

  _____

  _____

  _____

  _____

SITUATION NO. 7:

Another driver passed a red light and hit your car. (No one was injured.) The estimated cost of the car repair is $1,000. The insurance company offers you only $400 because, in their opinion, "It's an old car, and that's all it's worth."

Reaction/Action:

How do you get what you want?

- Shock! Disbelief! Anger! Frustration!
- Take the $400, and pay the additional $600 out of your pocket. You can't beat the insurance company anyway.
- Try to convince the insurance agent that you really need the $1,000.
- Talk to higher and higher levels of management, requesting the $1,000.
- Get the car fixed; pay the bill; and hope you can keep fighting with the insurance company.
- Don't get the car fixed (if that's possible for you to do), and keep demanding the $1,000.
- Contact the State Insurance Commission in your state, and prepare to file a complaint against the insurance company.
- Inform the insurance company of your contact with the State Commission. Wait for a response.
- If the insurance company sends you a check to cover what they feel is a "reasonable settlement" (In this case—$400), you have to decide if you will:
  A. Cash the check, and keep up the battle, or quit, or
  B. Don't cash the check, and keep up the battle. (Point of interest—The case can never be closed unilaterally by the insurance company. You must accept payment and cash the check, or the case

remains open. Another point—The longer you can hold out, the better your chances are to get a favorable settlement.)

- Hire a lawyer, and let her or him fight the insurance company for you.

- Other_____

_____

_____

_____

_____

Analysis:

- Which option is the best for you?_____

_____

- What tactics or strategies would you use?_____

_____

- What actions would you take?_____

_____

- Why?_____

_____

A Handy Form

When you face a confrontation, use this format to get ready. Fill in the blank spaces, and work out your options. Don't try to put them in any particular order at first. Just write down all of the possibilities that come to mind. This is an individual brainstorming session. The goal is to capture ideas as they are flowing, and not to evaluate them right away. That comes later. Make your own form in a notebook or on scrap paper, and use as much space as you need. A blank sample is provided on the following page.

Now it's all up to you. Good luck. Keep track of the "batting average" we discussed. You'll probably be surprised to see how well you do over time. And remember: practice, practice, practice, until winning is as natural as breathing.

In every conflict, at least one party is going to win—if you have the confidence, the plan, and the right strategy, it's going to be you!

SITUATION:

_____

_____

_____

_____

_____

Reaction/Action:

_____

_____

_____

_____

_____

Analysis:

- What option is the best for you?_____

  _____

- What tactics or strategies should you use?_____

  _____

- What actions should you take?_____

  _____

- Why?_____

  _____

  _____

  _____

70725

Notes

Notes

Notes

Notes

Notes

Notes